My Crazy Life

How I survived my family

My Crazy Life

How I survived my family

Compiled by **Allen Flaming** and **Kate Scowen**

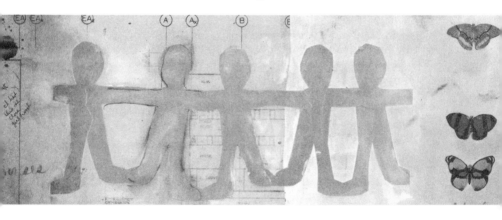

Annick Press
Toronto ✽ New York ✽ Vancouver

We acknowledge the support of the Canada Council for the Arts, the Ontario Arts Council, and the Government of Canada through the Book Publishing Industry Development Program (BPIDP) for our publishing activities.

The publisher wishes to express its gratitude to Carolyn Kennedy for her editorial contributions.

Cataloguing in Publication Data

Main entry under title:

My crazy life : how I survived my family

ISBN 1-55037-733-7 (bound).—ISBN 1-55037-732-9 (pbk.)

1. Teenagers—Family relationships—Case studies.
2. Problem families—Case studies.

HQ799.15.M92 2002   306.87   C2001-903236-6

The art in this book was rendered in mixed media.
The text was typeset in Apollo MT.

Distributed in Canada by: Published in the U.S.A. by Annick Press (U.S.) Ltd.
Firefly Books Ltd.   Distributed in the U.S.A. by:
3680 Victoria Park Avenue   Firefly Books (U.S.) Inc.
Willowdale, ON   P.O. Box 1338
M2H 3K1   Ellicott Station
                                Buffalo, NY 14205

Printed and bound in Canada by Friesens, Altona, Manitoba.

visit us at: **www.annickpress.com**

my family

ME

Contents

I had this one close girlfriend, but she was kind of screwed up too. She was always moving schools and her mother was a single parent we were really good friends

Acknowledgments

We would like to thank all those who have supported us, advised us, and contributed to this book. Our families demonstrated the patience and belief in our project that kept us moving ahead. Thanks to Grant, Hatley, Sydney, Quinn, Eve-Lynn, Zachary, and Janna.

It was Rick Wilks's expertise and enthusiasm that kept us going when it would have been all too easy to procrastinate for another day. His advice and encouragement kept us on track.

The stories in this book would not have come to light without the support of several community and social service agencies. They helped to identify and connect us with young people who were willing to talk about their lives and their families. In particular, we would like to thank Kate Thorpe from S.W.Y.M. and Bridget Sinclair from St. Stephen's Community House.

We would also like to thank all the youth who were interviewed for the book. We were unable to use all of their stories and it was difficult to choose among them. We truly admire their honesty and courage. Their experiences will undoubtedly be an inspiration for many others.

Allen Flaming and Kate Scowen

Introduction

Families can really make you crazy. Some have troubled people in them or face situations that make life especially difficult for their members. These are the families you will read about in this book. In each of these families there are kids, like you, who are struggling to make sense of the craziness. They have found ways to keep their lives on track despite what is going on around them. Each is dealing with what has happened to them in their own way. Their stories are sometimes frightening or sad, funny or heroic, but above all inspiring. We hope that by reading this book you will better understand your crazy family and learn how you too can survive.

In our work as professionals providing support to youth and families, we have met a lot of young people who faced really difficult times. Once they had a chance to sit down and talk about why they were failing at school, why they got arrested, or why they were hurting themselves, their stories often came around to their families and what was going on at home. We want our families to take care of us, and we expect the adults in our lives to be the sane, stable ones. But adults are people, just older versions of you. Some are messed up, some are ill, and some had equally crazy family lives when they were kids.

When we started this book we had an idea of the kinds of stories we thought we would hear: divorce, addictions, abuse, neglect. What surprised us was the way each kid handled his or her situation differently. Some, like Logan, dealt with their situation by becoming violent, getting into trouble, and using drugs. Some, like Aislin, channeled their anger and hurt in other directions, like art and sports. We have changed their names and the names of the

places where they live, work, and go to school to protect their privacy. But their stories are real: What each one said was that getting into trouble made it harder to get through those tough times. They told us that acting out, using drugs, or breaking the law almost always made things worse. Their advice: Even if it seems like the only way to go at the time, try to think about the consequences of what you are doing, for yourself and for others. When you've already been hurt, it doesn't help to punish yourself more by screwing up and getting in trouble. Of course, that's easy to say but hard to do when it's all coming down on you.

We hope that you somehow find this book at a point in your life when you can really use it. You may not totally identify with every story, but probably some of the situations, issues, and responses will ring true for you. If they do, we hope you can find some comfort and inspiration in knowing that other kids have lived through crazy times with their families and so you can too. Maybe these stories can help you to have a better understanding of who you are and give you more confidence to make the changes you need to live a healthier life. Be sure to check out the Afterword on page 123 to find out about places and people who can help you or connect you with services and support.

If you are a relative, friend, or counselor of someone having difficult times at home, we hope that these stories provide you with ideas as to how to help and support them. Remember that they need you to be there, even if sometimes they seem to be doing everything possible to distance themselves from everyone. Maybe you can be that one friend, teacher, or aunt who gives them the strength they need to survive their crazy families.

Allen Flaming and Kate Scowen
Toronto, Canada, November 2001

Cassandra

Cassandra sees herself as a "pleaser." She likes to see other people happy, but sometimes that means she gets caught up in their fights. Her parents split up when she was 13 and she often got drawn into their battles. When Mom started living with another woman and Dad started dating someone with kids Cassandra's age, she had to figure out how to relate to her new families. Her sister, Zoe, continues to look for that "perfect" family, but Cassandra knows their family will never return to the way it used to be when Mom, Dad, and the kids all lived together in one house.

The Split

I guess it started the spring I turned thirteen. I was sort of oblivious to events that happened before that because my parents had been breaking up and having problems in their relationship for at least three years. I didn't really clue in until then; it didn't seem that serious.

I think my parents separated because they were both growing, and changing, within themselves. My mother was in intensive therapy, trying to get over issues from her own childhood. That summer, my sister, Zoe, my dad, and I went out West to my uncle's wedding, and my mom didn't come with us. I sort of thought it was because she was starting school in September — that's what I told people — but I think it was really because she just didn't want to be with us.

So, in the month of August, she moved out. She had decided to move in with a friend for a month, to get some breathing space. She told Zoe and me she was leaving before she told my dad, while he was away. We were sitting in the living room, and I guess she had been hinting that there were problems, and then she said, "I still love you both, and Dad, he's a great man, but I just need some space right now."

She had been doing art therapy: she had this big painting with different characters that came out of it, different personalities, and she used that to describe the way she was feeling. I don't remember what exactly, but it was this whole process that helped her to realize something.

It was a bit weird, but I just stayed quiet and let it roll. I didn't interfere at all. I don't think my sister and I talked about it then. Zoe is two years older than me, but we didn't really talk much. I think she was upset, and I'm sure she talked to my mom about it.

My dad got back the next day, and he was really upset that Mom had told us before she told him. She said, "Well, I'm going to be living with Amy for a month..." and he just blew up. I remember being there with them and they were arguing. He was really angry with her and felt she was walking out on him, not giving him a chance.

At first I had thought leaving was just sort of a retreat for my mom, but seeing my dad afraid that she wouldn't come back was scary for me. He obviously knew more about their relationship than I did, and he had the impression she wouldn't want to return. But she did, this time, at least for a few months.

No One To Talk To

Then September came and Zoe and I had school. Seventh grade had been an okay time; I had friends and stuff. But my eighth-grade year just sort of fell apart for me. I lost all contact with friends. I don't know how. I think my personality changed and I became closed off from everyone, or maybe I stopped trusting people. I don't really know. But I just sort of kept to myself.

I didn't want to hang out with my friends, but they were also pretty mean to me that year. They always made fun of me. I had one close friend, who was kind of screwed up too. She was always changing schools; her mother was a single parent and she said her mom beat her up. She was kind of in control of our relationship, which was always off and on. But aside from her, I didn't have anyone I could confide in. I didn't like my teacher, so there wasn't anyone; it was really hard.

Zoe was in her junior year, and she went through sort of a weird down spell too; she started wearing all kinds of makeup, and she had crazy friends, and parties. It was hard for me to communicate with her because she was really rude and angry. So there was really no one I could talk to.

There were some family friends that I hung out with a lot. They had always been in my life because I grew up in their neighborhood. They sort of became like second parents to me. I was too shy to talk about the situation at home, though. They knew what was going on but I was sort of defensive about my parents, and I didn't want people to know about it. I was really shy and self-conscious, and I didn't have much self-esteem. I guess I just didn't want people to know.

Life At Mom's

My mom moved out for good on the 10th of December. It's funny: I remember the date but not the conversation we had when she told us. I think I didn't want to be involved so I tried to forget a lot of it. So I don't remember exactly how she found her new house, though I do remember looking with her. When we came to this house,

I hated it. It was dirty and gross, with shaggy carpets. The day she moved out, a friend of mine was having a birthday party and I had to say, "No, I can't go. My mom's having a moving-in party." We ripped up the gross flooring, and then we had really good food, and all my mom's friends were there, so it was like a celebration, almost.

We started right away with the one-week-on, one-week-off routine. At first we just slept on mattresses on the floor. My mom tried to set up rooms to make us feel comfortable, but it was a difficult period because we weren't really established there. The basement was unfinished and that's where my bedroom was supposed to be, so I was sleeping in the living room on a futon. Still, we got settled pretty quickly. I think we were pretty supportive of my mom and in turn she was supportive of us.

Life At Dad's

The alternate weeks we spent with my dad were difficult for all of us. My memory of this whole period is unclear. I think my sister and I were living on the third floor together, but then we had to rent it out because we didn't have my mom's income anymore. So that was a new beginning there: we moved down to new bedrooms on the second floor, and we had this lady living upstairs, who had to go through the house to get there.

My dad never talked about the separation. I think I always felt bad for him because he said, indirectly, that I was walking out on him. One day we were sitting on his bed talking and he was blaming her, and I thought, I want to talk to you but I can't because you're fighting her through me. It's always been difficult to talk to him about issues.

There were times when I wouldn't want to approach him about things because I knew he was angry. I guess I didn't like living there as much. It was still my home, and in a way it was where I was more comfortable, but he was touchier than my mom and I found it really hard to talk to him, especially if there was something wrong.

Mom Comes Out

About a year after the separation, my mom came out to me. We were sitting at the kitchen table in her house. I was fourteen, in ninth grade, and things were more settled by then. She had this friend who was around the house quite a bit and she introduced it by saying, "Jane is not just a friend to me."

I asked her, "Are you gay?"

And she said, "Yeah."

We talked for a while about when and how it had happened for her. I don't know how she realized it, or discovered it, but I don't think I took it hard. It was kind of cool. By that point I knew my parents were over and I was used to it. It wasn't like I thought they were ever going to get back together.

At first, though, seeing my mom and Jane together as a couple was definitely pretty weird. Just seeing her with another person was weird, though it was a lot easier that it was a woman; it was more comfortable. I didn't feel like I had to be reserved at home.

I remember walking in on them once. They weren't doing anything, but they were lying on the bed together and Jane didn't have a top on. I took off. But I didn't have to adjust to another male body, so it wasn't like she was replacing my father at all. I didn't feel like she was jeopardizing our family. She was nice, and reserved, but she had a lot of issues in her own family, and she had a six-year-old kid. There was talk of her moving in with us, but we didn't like the idea because her son would have moved in too and

we didn't like him. Jane's husband was really aggressive and abusive, and so was her son. He bossed us around and we thought, there's no way we're living with him.

I don't know if my mom told my dad that she was gay, or if it was Zoe. I wanted to hide it from him. I knew it would be hard for him and I didn't want to be the one to break it to him. But he didn't react that much to her coming out. If you asked, he would say it was private. But once he referred to my mom's girlfriend as her "plaything," or some other mean name, and I thought, Whoa! That's not okay. She's my mother. You can't fight her through me just because you are angry.

He apologized, but he said those were his feelings. It made it hard that he couldn't talk to her. Communication skills were really lacking between them. They didn't fight that much, but they resorted to e-mail to avoid talking to each other. They couldn't detach from each other completely, because of the joint custody, but they didn't want to talk. Sometimes we'd forget to pass a message, and we'd get blamed.

Dad Starts Dating

My dad started dating again but he didn't talk about it much. He'd just say, "I'm going to a movie with a friend of mine." I remember meeting one woman. She came out with us on a Sunday, and we went for a walk in the park. She was a nice person but it was a weird situation. It was never official and my dad wasn't affectionate with her. It wasn't like they were dating; it was like they were friends. It didn't last.

I think it was the following fall (I'm not really sure because my dad never said anything) that he went to the Western Counties for a while. He was mountain-biking in this little town and he went to a pub to have dinner. A

woman asked to sit down beside him and he said sure, and after that they became friends.

Now my dad is doing his sabbatical in her town, to be near her. They're going to move in together. We went to visit them a couple of months after they met. Danielle has an eighteen-year-old and a sixteen-year-old, which fits perfectly with Zoe and me. It was strange because we would be left alone with her kids and we'd talk about it, stuff like "Does your mom date very much?"

It's nice now, though. Her daughter is living with us here. She just finished her degree and she's working with my dad at the university. We've become close, even though we don't see each other very much.

I see Danielle when she visits here. And my dad goes there, every two weeks or so. I've always liked her being around because it raised his spirits, so it was easy to get used to her being here. She makes him happy, and I like everybody to be happy. I'm sort of a pleaser.

I think my mom was happy about my dad's relationship too. She felt it was better for us kids that he was happier, so she didn't object to it. She was the one who didn't want to be with him anymore, so she said, "Good for him." She'd talk about it like she was our girlfriend. It's a lot easier to talk openly to my mom.

Another New Face

So we got used to Danielle and Jane. But then Jane started cheating on my mother. My mom didn't know it for a while, and Jane was a wreck and didn't know how to tell her. They had been together for about a year when they broke up. It was hard on my mom because it had been a pretty intense relationship. She grieved for a while, but she knew how to get over it, and she did.

There are a lot of changes happening again now. It

started one night when we were having a dinner party and my mom's friend Jill came over. Things started happening with them. That's going well and they're moving in together. They bought a cottage at Lake Washington and they'll be up there three or four times a week.

But there have been a lot of issues with Jill for Zoe and me. Jill's very authoritative and respect-oriented, and Zoe and I have problems with that. Last summer we went on a camping trip for a couple of days, and this weird thing happened. We were driving, and I tossed a pillow into the front seat. It hit Jill and she got upset about it; she felt that it was disrespectful. I was dumbfounded at that, but Jill felt I was trying to tell her something. She didn't really say anything to me, but she talked to my mom about it and then my mom got really upset.

I said I was sorry, but her reaction seemed bizarre to me. Jill said that if someone had done that to her mother's friend when she was a kid, it would have been really bad. My mom didn't get mad at me; she explained to Jill that we weren't used to such reactions and tried to help her through it. But they started arguing, and we had to stop the car and talk about it. Jill threatened to return home; she said, "You don't want me here." I felt incredibly bad. I didn't know what to do. Zoe wondered where Jill's reaction came from too.

We carried on with the trip, but at the campsite we had this whole other blow-up. We were playing miniature golf. Jill and I were both tense, and we were snapping at each other, making little comments here and there. My mom was getting really angry because she was in the middle of it. Then we locked ourselves out of the car and we all had different opinions about how to get it open again. Jill wouldn't let me try my idea; she felt I was being really pushy.

That's when it just blew up again. We got in a huge fight and started packing up to leave. Jill thought I was rude and disrespectful to her, and she thought Zoe and I were rude and disrespectful to each other. It was really crazy and I felt so angry. And it was hard for my mom, being in the middle.

Jill had never said anything before, but there she was saying stuff like, you kids are really rude. So my mom said, "If that's the way you feel, we can't be together. You're going to have to take a bus home. I can't tolerate this anymore." We drove back together, though, still snapping at each other. We stopped at a coffee place, and the snapping continued, so my mom left us all in the car. I apologized to Jill for my reaction, but I said that I couldn't help feeling she was out of line. We resolved it temporarily then, but it was only the beginning of this whole thing between us. It was supposed to be a family weekend for us, but the way it worked out told us we weren't ready for that yet. We didn't know Jill very well then. Maybe we felt some resentment about her being in the family.

That was last summer. Since then, it has been a long, gradual process of working it out, of learning to understand each other and to respect each other's boundaries and privacy. Now, we're more comfortable with each other — obviously, as she's moving in. I'm adjusting, and it's better now.

Looking Back

I think I played a role in the family: the peacekeeper, the cheerer-upper, the positive energy. But at the same time, I was often too shy to get involved. My sister used to fight when my parents were fighting. She would get into the arguments to try to make them stop, or she'd just yell and scream and cry. I sort of sat on the sidelines and watched.

Or I'd try to say, "Zoe, it's okay," but she'd fight me off. She didn't want that comfort from me. I think I felt out of place. I felt alone and I didn't want to get involved with my parents or my sister fighting.

At my mom's house, she sort of tried to nurture me while I was getting used to things. I don't know what my role was there. At my dad's place, I tried to make people happy. I think that's what I always did.

At school, too, I tried to make my friends like me. It was hard, but I think the only thing I've really kept from that time is that I'm still sort of self-conscious and I want people to like me and appreciate me. I didn't feel appreciated at home because I wasn't in the spotlight: there were lots of other things my parents were dealing with. Zoe got attention by yelling and screaming; then she also started stealing a bit and got into trouble at school.

I concentrated on getting good marks and playing sports. I started playing hockey; that's probably what I focused on. I liked being with the boys. There were eight or nine of us on the team, and we got to know each other pretty well. That was nice because I felt like I had an attachment, and some friends. I had always played sports, like softball. I did my schoolwork, and I became really organized and always cleaned my room: I became a neat freak. I was the good girl. I didn't get involved very much, and I didn't have friends over. I just tried to do everything well.

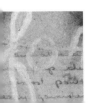

Peter

Peter lived on the streets for more years than he cares to remember. Before that he was in and out of a series of foster homes, cousins' homes, and girlfriends' apartments. Feelings of betrayal by his alcoholic father and abandonment by his mother have always dogged him. He turned to theft, drugs, and alcohol for some sort of direction. Now he thinks he's found the key: find the right friends, talk about what's bothering you, and get in touch with loved ones before it's too late.

Life Without Mom

Life with my family was hard. My dad was an alcoholic. Originally, there was my mom, my dad, my older sister, and me. My parents split up when I was two, though, and I grew up with my dad and my stepmother. There's a lot of stuff from my childhood that I don't remember. I remember most of the bad stuff, but the good stuff hasn't come back to me.

My mom's explanation for why my dad raised us was that she couldn't support us, so she gave us to him. My dad's story was a bit different. He said he came home from work one day and found my sister and me in a cold bathtub, and my mom wasn't there, so he took us. I don't know which is true. I don't remember. My sister probably does, but she won't tell me anything. Neither will my mom. I can't ask my dad because he's dead.

I think the problems really started when I was six or seven. One night my mom dropped us off at my dad's on her way to work. But instead of coming to the door with

us, she waited in the car until we were let in, and then she left. My stepmom didn't like that. She waited until my mom got home, and then she phoned and told her she wasn't allowed to see us anymore. For eight years after that, I didn't get to see my mom. I never forgave my dad and stepmom for that.

When I was told that I couldn't see my mom, I decided I didn't want to be at my dad's anymore, so I started running away from home. I would go to friends' places, or walk around the town, anything to avoid being at home, because my dad was an alcoholic.

I was always getting grounded, or getting the belt, just for stupid things. I was always getting in trouble, even for things I didn't do. For example, my sister used to steal things from my dad and stepmom and I would get blamed. She mostly stole candy, or money. One time she stole cigarette butts. That was funny. I was mad at her so I told them that she was smoking the butts. My dad made her sit down and smoke a whole cigar so she would get sick and stop smoking. It didn't work though; she still smokes.

Back then, my sister and I used to talk a lot, even though I didn't really understand what was going on. We were really close at one point in time, but that changed, I guess.

I couldn't accept my stepmom as my mother because I already had a mother. I didn't want another one. But it had more to do with her. She had my dad wrapped around her little finger. Anything she said, went.

I hardly got to see my dad when I was a kid. He was a truck driver, so he was hardly home. He would be gone for three weeks, home for a week, then gone again for weeks. Life was horrible when he was gone. Everything I did was wrong, and my stepmom made sure to tell me. From the time I was a little kid, I had to make my bed, wash dishes, clean. She called me names, called me a rotten

child, things like that. My dad didn't know what was going on until he got home and she would fill him in.

My dad and my stepmom were always fighting because of his drinking. They would yell and things would start flying. I left the house once because they were fighting and went next door to a friend of theirs. I can't remember his name now, but he knew what was going on and he would take me in.

I was a really bad kid, though. I used to go missing from school. I failed grade one because I threw something at my French teacher. I missed her by an inch. I had a bad temper when I was a kid. I still do, but I've got it under control now.

There wasn't anybody at school I could talk to. I didn't have many friends. I didn't want any. I thought everybody was better than me, so I just wanted to be left alone. I used to get into a lot of fights in elementary school, for no reason. Somebody would just look at me the wrong way and I'd be in a bad mood, and we'd just start.

A lot of my anger came from the environment I was growing up in at home. It wasn't fun. I missed a lot of my childhood because of it. I was abused mentally, physically, and sexually — it all happened. I know about the sexual abuse from my stepsister, but I just don't want to remember it. There are certain parts of my childhood that I just can't remember. I never told anyone about the sexual abuse until years and years later.

Life Without Dad

I don't know if it was a teacher or the principal (they all knew what was going on) who called the Children's Aid Society, but I was put in the Children's Aid when I was about eleven. The social worker asked if I wanted to stay at home or if I'd rather live somewhere else. I told her I didn't

want to be at home anymore. So I packed up my stuff and went to a foster home for six months. I loved it; they were great people. They took me camping and gave me an allowance. They had other foster kids there too.

I talked to my dad once or twice during that time, and I went home to visit, but it wasn't great, because of his alcoholism. He would get really stupid when he was drunk and sometimes he was violent. I've been banged off of walls and kicked up a flight of stairs. He was like that with my sister for a while too, but then he just took it all out on me. There was nothing my stepmother could do when he was like that. She'd just tell him to sit down and shut up and go to sleep. Sometimes he would.

After six months, I was given another choice: either go back and live with my dad or go to my cousin Rick's. So I chose to go to my cousin's. I didn't know him well, but I didn't want to go back to my dad's.

My cousin Rick taught me a lot about myself. I lived with him, his girlfriend, and her two kids. The daughter was around my age. The son was older than I was, in high school. It was mostly fun. Sure, there were rules I had to follow, and I got in trouble sometimes, but they lived in the country, just outside of Akron, and I loved it. It was an awesome little place. I went to school, and things were a bit better with friends. I didn't get in so many fights. I played a lot of baseball and did other sports while I was there. It was really fun. I lived there for four years, until I was fifteen. I still had contact with my dad; I would call him, or go see him. I wasn't getting any counseling by then and the Children's Aid was out of the picture completely.

Mom Returns

One day, close to the end of the school year when I was fifteen, I was sitting at home when my sister phoned and

said, "Guess what? I found Mom!" I don't know how she found her, though I know she phoned my mom and met up with her before she even told me.

She gave me my mom's number and I called her. It was kind of awkward. I hadn't seen her for eight years. I didn't know what to say. I made arrangements to go see her, but I didn't know what I was going to do during the visit. I didn't know what to expect. I cried a lot when I went there. She lived in Marystown. She came to Akron to see me, took me out to dinner and took me shopping. We visited back and forth after that.

At my eighth-grade graduation, just after meeting my mom, I found out that my cousin Rick and his family were moving to California. They asked whether I wanted to move with them or go live with my mom. What a decision! There I was, just getting ready to go to high school, and they threw this at me. It was one of the hardest decisions I've had to make in my life. I was really attached to them, but, at the same time, I had just found my mom.

I decided to move in with my mom. It was a decision that turned out to be both good and bad. My mom didn't know how to raise a teenager, and I didn't listen; I didn't like authority. I still don't. I listened better when I was at Rick's because there weren't all the bad influences; I actually had good influences when I lived there. But that all changed when I moved to the city to live with my mom.

My dad knew I had moved in with my mom, but he didn't say much about it. He never did say much when it came to her. My stepmom couldn't say anything either because I hadn't been living with them when I moved to my mom's. I wouldn't have let her tell me what to do at that point anyway. I was pretty much old enough to make my own decisions.

I like small towns, so moving to Marystown was a

really big change. There was a lot more to do and more people to meet. I was just starting high school, but instead of becoming a leader I became a follower. I got into all sorts of trouble. I started stealing, smoking marijuana, and drinking. School just wasn't fun. I found it boring. I think that's why I had so much trouble. I wasn't doing any of the sports I had been doing in Akron. I tried football but I didn't like it. After a while I gave up and dropped out of school.

My mom lived with her partner, Ken. They've been together now for twelve or thirteen years. I got a job through Ken, doing landscaping at this complex where he was superintendent. I picked up all the garbage outside, cut the grass, and planted flowers, trees and shrubs. It was good; it gave me some money. Then I got stupid and spent it all on drugs, alcohol, food, and friends. I didn't care.

Not Talking

I don't know what I was feeling all those years. I think I just shut off a lot of the feelings. I didn't want to deal with them. I never really had an outlet. I couldn't talk to my dad. It would have broken his heart if I had ever told him how I really felt, though I think he may have known a bit. Not all of it, but a little.

I had always wondered where my mom was and what she was doing with her life. I never asked her where she had been for those eight years I hadn't seen her. But I thought about it. I wondered why she had given us up, why she didn't want to see me anymore. After a while, though, I just stopped thinking about it.

My relationship with my sister was one where she did most of the talking, and I just listened. She used to pour her heart out to me all the time. I didn't really understand what she said but I felt that I was doing good, and she needed somebody to listen to her, so I did. I didn't have

anyone to listen to me. I just bottled it up and got angry.

I guess I got mad at her too. One day we were downstairs playing and she threw something at me. I had this little toy spaceship that you wound up and it would fly. But this time I didn't wind it up, I just chucked it like a Frisbee and it cut her face. It could have blinded her. Boy, did I ever get in trouble from my dad and stepmom. I got the belt, as usual, and I was grounded. My sister needed two or three stitches, and she stayed mad at me for a while.

I had a lot of extended family: my grandparents, and lots of aunts, uncles, and cousins, all on my dad's side. I've never met any of my mom's family because she's from out East. I guess they're all out there. I've never heard my mom talk about them.

My grandparents were great. I loved my grandfather; he taught me how to whistle. I got to see him regularly and he spent a lot of time with me. After I moved to my cousin's, I didn't see as much of my grandparents but I still got to go there for Christmas and stuff.

Even though I had a great relationship with my grandfather, I never talked to him about what was going on at home. I don't know if he knew what went on there or not. My grandmother might have known — she was a pretty smart lady — but she didn't say anything. She could sense things though. She knew if something was wrong. You could try to hide it all you wanted, but she'd just keep at you until you told her what was bothering you. But I never poured my heart out to her.

My grandma loved to cook. I'm a good cook now and I think that's where I learned. I used to help her bake pies and cakes and cookies, and help her with the big dinners she always cooked. Visiting there was great fun. I miss those times.

Out on the Street

So I lived with my mom for about a year and a half, until one long weekend, when she and Ken went away, I decided to have a party. I broke into the liquor cabinet and we took every drop, including their wine collection. My mom's room was broken into during the party too and things were stolen. I knew who had the stuff, so I got most of it back later. At the time I tried to make it look like a break-in, but it didn't work and I got caught.

My mom was really, really mad. She gave me two weeks to get out of her house, and she called the cops on me. That was the first time I was arrested. I was charged with public mischief, and I got probation, which was no big deal. I was really mad at my mom at the time for kicking me out and having me arrested. But then I got to thinking, wait a minute, it's not her fault, it's mine. I was the one who was stupid, not her. So I forgave her.

After I got kicked out I went to a shelter in Marystown. I think one of the workers from school hooked me up with that. It was good. That first time, I was there for about a month and a half. Then I left and just went from friend's place to friend's place. Even though there were workers at the shelter, all the other kids there looked up to me. There was one kid who called me Dad. I almost smacked him. I told him I wasn't his father and that he shouldn't call me that. I was helping them and helping myself at the same time. I was giving them advice, and saving bits and pieces of it to use on myself. I'm still the same way. I'd rather help everybody else than help myself. That's just the way I am. I really didn't care about myself. Even now, I still try to help people out. It's just my nature, I guess. I know how it feels to have a rough childhood.

After being on the street for a while, I went back to the shelter. At this point, I was becoming an alcoholic, like my dad; I was drinking heavily and I didn't care. I wasn't violent back then, but I didn't want to end up like my father, so I went to Alcoholics Anonymous. I was about seventeen. I stayed with AA until I got my first badge. I didn't go back after that. I didn't need to. I only drink occasionally now. It's not a problem.

I wasn't working when I was drinking heavily. I got money from my mom, and the shelter gave us a personal-needs allowance, so that's how I bought booze. I was still in contact with my mom, and she gave me half of her family assistance check whenever I needed the money. But when I found out she could get in trouble for collecting assistance when I wasn't living with her, I told her to send the next check back.

I visited my dad once when I was living at the shelter. At one point during the visit he was going to hit my sister. I had just had it. You don't go hitting my sister, or any females, around me. I'd seen enough of that as a kid. So I told him to sit down and shut up or I'd throw him out the window. So he sat down, and then he passed out.

The second time I got arrested, I hadn't even done anything. It was because of this guy who decided he was going to steal a pair of rollerblades, in his knapsack. My buddy and I were looking for something to buy his girl-friend. We didn't buy anything, but as we walked out of the store the other guy came out right behind us and a security guard nabbed all of us. I got charged with theft under a thousand dollars.

The third time, I was keeping liquor for a friend of mine. He decided to be stupid and go rob portables. So he broke in. I don't think he even had time to steal anything. Some guy was walking by and he caught us. I could have left but I didn't want to leave my friend. I took the rap for it and went to jail for a week. I was eighteen, so I wasn't in juvenile detention anymore. It made me realize I didn't want to be in that position again, and I haven't been since. I can't be bothered. There are too many things to do with my life besides going to jail.

Moving Around

By this point, I wasn't talking to any of my family and I was planning to move to Columbus with a girl. I called my family before I left because I figured my mom and my sister were worried about me. Big mistake. I got yelled at and told that I should have gone back to my mom's. I promised I would call again within a couple of weeks, but I didn't call for a few months. I'm famous for that. I was always pulling disappearing acts on my family. I'm used to just up and leaving. I could be back in a week, or a month, or a year. Who knows? I'll be back when I'm back. They never knew where I was, even when I was little.

I stayed in Columbus for about six months. I was working, and then I went on welfare again. The girl I was with decided she didn't want to be with me anymore. We had been going out for a year and a half when she came to me one day and said she needed space. The first thing I did was ask her who the new guy was. She said there wasn't anybody else. So I told her to take her space. She said she was moving out, so I again asked who she was seeing, but she wouldn't tell me. I already had a suspicion it was a guy from work.

I came back to Marystown because of my sister. She's married, but she's not with her husband anymore. She wanted to see me for Christmas. At first I didn't want to — something was telling me to just stay away — but I came anyway. She took me for all my money and basically left me high and dry. I ended up buying things for her until I was broke, and, meanwhile, she had money. She said she

would pay me back, so I was stuck in her apartment, babysitting her kids. I couldn't go out and look for work or a place to live.

Then somebody phoned the Children's Aid Society on her and I had to deal with them. I told them she treated her kids well. I said that I came over in the mornings to babysit so she could go to work, and that I went home at night, because I didn't want them to know I was living at my sister's. So she still has the kids. She was working at Value Mart at the time. I never got any money from her. Eventually, they moved out and I ended up on the streets again.

I still talk to my sister, but I won't live with her. She's living with my aunt now, my stepmother's sister. I lived with her too before, for seven months. She put up my bond and I had to live with her. She wouldn't allow me to smoke or go to the mall, I couldn't see my friends, I had to go to school, and I had to clean the house, a three-bedroom house with a basement, from top to bottom, by myself.

Losing Dad

Last June, on his birthday, my dad had a heart attack and died. He would have been sixty. I think it was the alcohol that killed him. My stepmom died just a few weeks after he did. She had diabetes, and I think she also had cancer.

I didn't see my dad before he died. I didn't know where he was at that point, and I didn't really care. Now I regret it. I had actually been thinking of reconciling with him. I wanted to say things to him that I had never had the chance to say. I would have told him I was sorry for hurting him, back when I was always running away from home. Regardless of what he did to me, he was my dad and I loved him. I wish I had him back in my life. I never got the chance to explain to him why I did the things I did.

My sister was the one who told me my dad had died. I didn't find out until after the funeral. He had been cremated. Now my stepsister has his ashes.

I did go to my stepmom's funeral. It was okay, until I broke down and cried. But I still couldn't forgive her. That was something I could never do. I could never forgive my dad either. They took my mother away. If they hadn't taken me away from my mother, I don't think I would have gone through a lot of what I went through.

I'm still in contact with my mom. I call her once or twice a week. But I don't visit and I can't live there. Ken won't let me in the house because of what happened when I stole all the booze. He's still holding a grudge. I want to show him that I've grown up, that I'm not the little brat I once was, that I'm an adult. But he won't let it go. I still haven't even talked to him.

Looking Back

I did think my family was nuts when I was growing up. That's why I've walked away from them. I remember thinking, what the hell am I here for? Do I even belong to this family? I wondered if I was adopted. When I was younger, my dad told me I wasn't his son. That hurt. All my life, my family put me down and told me I'd go nowhere, told me that I was stupid.

I don't think anyone understood me. Even today, I don't think people understand me. I tell them that I'm a complex person and it will take a while to get to know me. I can shut anybody out anytime I want. I can just snap my fingers and they don't exist anymore. I can be very cold when I want to, and I think it's just because of my upbringing. I practically had to raise myself, when I was a kid. I had to do chores, and I had to grow up fast. I didn't have time to be a child.

When I first moved back in with my mom, she thought I was stupid. She sent me to see this shrink-type person at the school, and they ran a test on me, some math and English questions. About halfway through, they gave me a puzzle. I couldn't put it together, no matter how I tried, so I picked it up and threw it across the room. I got up to leave and the doctor said we weren't done yet. I told her to evaluate me on whatever portion I had already done, and I left. My mom wasn't too happy, but I didn't care because she had forced me to do something I didn't want to do. The puzzle had made me angry because it was so frustrating. No matter which way I looked at it, the pieces just wouldn't go together.

Recently, both my grandparents have died, first my grandfather, then my grandmother. That was really hard, especially losing my grandfather. I didn't get to see my grandmother before she died, but I went to both of their funerals. My grandfather left me an old rifle that my aunt tried to get me to sell to her. I said no. I wanted to remove the firing pin, get it plugged and make sure it couldn't be fired, and mount it on a wall. She said she'd hang onto it until I was old enough to have it, but then she sold it without even telling me.

After the Craziness

My life finally seems to be getting better. I'm used to all these doors slamming in my face, but lately doors have been opening up. I'm too overwhelmed to choose though. I went through a youth employment program, so I can always go back and talk to a counselor to sort stuff out.

I have a good job right now. I hope I can keep it. I might go back to school for my high school diploma, but I'd rather have a degree or a certificate. I could show it to people and say, "I didn't finish high school, and look what

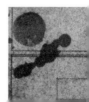

I've got!" Right now, though, I just want to get settled, then worry about school.

It has taken me a while to get here. When I first hit the streets, man, I was scared. But I got in with *some* of the right people and they helped me along the way. I've been lucky. I've had a lot of good friends. They've helped me through a lot. But I've done the same for them. I've come a long way.

Sometimes I sit back and I'm amazed at how far I've come, how I've gotten here from where I was, and all the little steps it took to get me here. Some of the values from some of the people I lived with must have rubbed off on me. People like my grandfather. He was quite a character.

The advice I'd give a kid growing up in a similar situation would be: Get help! Find someone you can talk to before it's too late. That's what a lot of the kids on the streets don't realize. They do have a place to go. They don't need to be on the streets. It's a lot tougher there than it is at home. It's especially hard in the winter; it gets really cold and it's not fun getting kicked out of parks and stuff.

There are places kids can go for help, but a lot of kids won't go to them because they're afraid. They don't want to take that step. The first major step is acknowledging that there is a problem. Then you have to admit that you need to get help.

I hope my story will help someone else. It has before. I stopped a fifteen-year-old from committing suicide. She had been raped, so she decided she was going to end it. I lost it. I looked at her and said: "You're only fifteen years old. You've got your whole life ahead of you. There are places you can go to get help. So use them!" And she did.

Wanda

Wanda's first six years were the best years of her life. She was raised by her grandmother in Hungary, who gave her uncondi-tional love and planted a precious seed of hope in her. At six, her parents took her to the Netherlands and then to Canada, ripping her away from the best home she had known. In Canada, her mother seemed to have a lot of problems and took them out on Wanda by physically beating her. When the kids at school started ganging up on her and making her life miserable, she became very sad and started to hurt herself. Her advice to kids going through rough times is to stick with it; better times will eventually come if you have hope!

A Crazy Mom

I was born in Hungary and I lived with my dad's mom until I was six. She was like no other person I've ever met in my life. She had the biggest heart of gold. I was a very ener-getic child, maybe even a brat, but she never punished me physically. To discipline me, she'd just sit me down and talk to me in a calm, soft voice.

I didn't see much of my parents in those first six years. My dad was in the United States and my mom was somewhere in Hungary. They were trying to make money so they could move to the Netherlands and then immigrate to Canada. My mom would come to see me and spend time with me, but when I think of a bonding feeling, I think of my grandma. To this day, I don't know how often my mom visited. She says she was there all the time but I just don't remember her being there very often.

At six, I finally moved with my parents to the Netherlands. It was brutally hard to leave my grandma. This was my first experience of living with my mom and dad. When I lived with my grandparents, I remember understanding the notion of parents — I knew that other kids had moms and dads, and I knew I had a mom and dad — but it wasn't totally real somehow. It was exciting to think about going to live with my mom and dad, but there was this incredible confusion because I knew I would be losing my relationship with my grandma.

In the Netherlands I had to get used to living with my parents under insane conditions. At first they were renting a room in somebody's house, but since we were trying to get into Canada as refugees, we had to move to a refugee camp. All the people waiting to immigrate had to live in these portable huts at refugee camps while they waited for the paperwork to be processed.

One night I was in the kitchen with my mother and she suddenly blew up at me and slapped me across the face, really hard. I don't remember what I had done or said but I remember being so confused as to why my own mother would slap me. It was the first of many things to come that I wouldn't understand. So already I was confused about things like family structure and where we were going to be living. But I was still a kid, so little things could amuse me and I found happiness in things I'd never seen before. For example, I remember being excited because the Netherlands had Lego and Hungary didn't.

We were in the Netherlands for six months before we moved to Canada, and during that time I turned seven. That's when I really began to discover my mother. She had what I later learned was some kind of chemical imbalance. She was an extremely nervous, emotional person; if something went wrong, she would explode into

hysterical fits and just go crazy.

She subjected me to a lot of physical abuse. She would have these fits and become extremely violent. She did everything from dragging me across the floor by my hair to hitting me again and again. She didn't have any control. She would trash my room, then tell me to clean up the mess, or call me names that made me feel like crap. Once she started, she never censored the words she used with me. I was discovering my feminine qualities and I liked to play dress-up and flaunt myself a bit. Anytime I did it, though, I'd get the feeling from my mother that I was a slut.

My father, who is the greatest man in the world, really loved my mom, because they had gone through all the immigration stuff together. I would try to tell him that there was something really wrong with her. I think he was aware of how she was abusing me, but, unfortunately, he had a block of his own and wasn't ready to deal with it.

Sometimes, if the abuse happened when he was at home, he would try to help. He was very calm, so he wouldn't shout at her. He would quietly say: "You need to calm down. Why are you shouting? Why are you crying? Why are you throwing things? Just stop." That would make her more crazy, having her actions pointed out to her. But eventually she would calm down, and the whole thing would be swept under the rug. No one ever talked about it afterward.

Every once in a while my grandparents would call and I'd get to talk to my grandma. I also wrote her letters but it wasn't the same. It was difficult for me to be honest with her. There were so many times I just wanted to tell her about my mother.

In fact, I think my strong relationship with my grandmother was one of the reasons my mother was so

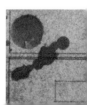

rotten to me. There must have been some sort of trigger about my having lived with my dad's family that caused her to feel such anger towards me. I got the feeling she was very defensive about not having been there when I was really young.

My mother would tell my grandmother that she didn't need to be told how to raise me. I think she hated that I had completely bonded with my grandmother, and instead of facing it and dealing with it she vented her feelings on me.

I never said anything to her about her absence during those years. Sometimes, in casual conversations about my early childhood, she would reminisce about sweet little things she said she remembered about me. I just let her do it. I never, ever, let her know how I really felt. I couldn't bring myself to say to her face, "You know what, bitch? I've never forgotten and will never feel towards you the way you want me to." To this day, I've never said those words to her.

Living in Terror

In Victoria, I was very isolated. I felt different from the other kids, and they often made fun of me. I constantly felt like I was missing something that everybody else seemed to have. I tried so hard to figure it out, but I couldn't. I lived in my room, where I had some space of my own, and I found joy in little things, like my toys. I talked to my dolls a lot. I couldn't speak English, so I had no friends and they had to put me back in kindergarten instead of grade one.

My dad was an engineer, so we had to move to wherever his work took him. We moved so many times. We lived in several different neighborhoods in Victoria, and then we moved to Calgary. I think I went to eleven or twelve schools, so I was always the new kid. I never made

any permanent friends or belonged to any group.

We lived in one neighborhood that was 90-per-cent black and Filipino. I really stuck out because I was one of the few white girls. At the elementary school, where I was the new girl again, the children were relentless in trying to crush somebody. There was no mercy in that school. I tried to fit in but they'd pretend to be my friend one day, then the next day they'd say they were going to beat me up after school. It was the girls at the school who tormented me, not the guys. I was terrified.

On one occasion, I went outside in the schoolyard and there were about twenty of them waiting for me. I came out and just started walking away, but they followed me and got in my face, trying to get me to fight them. I told them I wouldn't, that I was a small girl and there was no way I could fight them. They followed me all the way home, throwing snowballs at me on the street, humiliating me in public. When I got home and opened the door, they threw snowballs right into my house. I was hiding behind the door, thinking I just couldn't take it anymore, when my mother came down the stairs, screaming. She swung the door open, saw all those girls standing out there, and screamed and swore at them and threatened to call the school and get them suspended.

She did call and some of them did get suspended. I didn't feel that she was doing anything special for me, though. The suspensions didn't make me happy. I was worried about going back to school the next day. Now they had a real reason to hate me.

I couldn't go out for recess or lunch break at all. So I started helping the secretaries: answering the phones while they were at lunch, or restocking the storage room at recess. All the teachers and the principal knew what was going on. They talked to the other students and tried to get

them to leave me alone. No one could put their finger on what the problem was, on why everybody had this thing about me, because I hadn't done anything to them. I didn't have a single friend. Nobody ever stood up for me when all this stuff was going on.

One day, I went out at recess and just stood against the wall. I tried to find a corner where I could see everything but nobody could see me. It didn't work. One group noticed me and started calling me names. Even though this was a regular occurrence, that day something inside of me just snapped, and I exploded. I started screaming. I ran as fast as I could around the school, slammed through the front doors and into the office, threw everything off the secretary's desk and started stomping on it. I screamed that I couldn't take it anymore. I pulled my hair, bit the paper, did all this crazy stuff. The principal had to come out and talk to me until I calmed down.

After that, the principal decided we were going to have to have sessions. But they never called a social worker, or did anything else to get support for me. So I couldn't really depend on them to help me get through it.

Then one day, I was hiding in the bathroom and this big girl came in. She was a bit of an oddball too, but she was really smart and did well in school, so her head was on a little straighter than everyone else's. She asked me why I was hiding there. I told her I couldn't go out. She said, "You know what? You're going outside. You're going to go outside with *me!*"

So I went outside with her, and after that we became friends. It was amazing. It was kind of up and down, because then the other kids would start talking about her, but they wouldn't pick on her because she was pretty tough. She provided me with a little protection. She was my first little glimmer of hope *ever*.

I tried reaching out to some of the teachers at the school, but they didn't help. I once had a teacher who was Hungarian too. He was a great guy and a good teacher, but it was hard for him to keep the class under control. He was aware of what was going on at school with me. One day, something — I can't remember what — happened in the schoolyard, and everybody went back to class after recess, but I couldn't go in. I stayed in the hallway beside the door, bawling. So he told the class that whatever they were doing to me just had to stop.

Then he came out to the hallway and asked me to come inside. I remember looking at his face, trying to find something. I didn't know the words to use, but I wanted to just demand that he get me some peace. Whether from the principal or a teacher, I just wanted some peace. He couldn't give it to me.

Fighting Back

After my experiences in that school, I changed completely. I became really introverted. I started dressing all in black and became utterly negative. By then I was about twelve, and the love from my grandmother was running out. I wanted to kill myself. I started being very aggressively angry. I shaved half my head, began wearing black eyeliner, and argued with my parents all the time. Things got worse than ever between my mother and me. I was getting older and stronger. She was still violent with me.

There was one night when I was on the phone with a boy I had met. I was thirteen. My dad came into the room and, without saying a word, took the phone from me and hung it up. We argued, and he started shouting at me. Then my mom came into the room and started shouting at me. This time it was *both of them*! They both just started giving it to me physically, punching me. They got so riled

up. I was falling back on my bed but they wouldn't stop hitting me.

I know I wasn't easy to live with at that point. I was so negative because I had been crapped on so constantly and had started to take it out on my parents. But my *dad* hitting me: it was shattering. We had always had a good relationship. That's when I realized I must have done something *so* bad — not only did I know I sucked, but I was bad enough to have even found a weak point in my father!

When they stopped beating me, I got up and ran downstairs, grabbed my knapsack and threw some stuff into it, and ran out of the house. I just kept running, not knowing where I was going. I went to some guy's house, a complete delinquent I had met at school. But my parents somehow got his number and phoned his house. He freaked out because I was there and my parents were telling him they were going to call the police if I didn't go home. I was in complete chaos in my head. I didn't know what I was doing. I knew I didn't want to go back.

I ended up leaving his house and going over to this girl's house near my parent's place. Her parents called my parents and it was decided that I would spend the night there and my parents agreed not to call the police.

I went home after school the next day. We all sat down to eat dinner, with my mom struggling to stay contained. She couldn't even discuss it, because as soon as she started saying anything to me she knew she'd start losing it. There was so much tension in the air, it was ridiculous.

My dad started the conversation by telling me that I could never, ever, do that again. I replied that he could never, ever, touch me again. That's when my mom lost it. There are buttons in her that she knows about but will never face. You can press those buttons because she's got them exposed. If she could just deal with them, then she

wouldn't be this bomb about to go off all the time. She yelled, "Who do you think you are? You can't do this! I can't take it anymore!" I said something really bad back. My dad got up and threw me off the chair and told me I couldn't eat with them, that I had to sit in the living room. With my dad, though, the physical abuse was a one-time thing, and I understood it because I had provoked it.

Ways of Coping

I was always writing, keeping a journal, drawing, and doing schoolwork. I read a lot of books. I always had to document my existence. I needed a physical record of it. If I was really experiencing some crazy emotions, it wasn't enough to tell someone about it. I wanted to document it, to bring it to life. I wanted to know who else felt this, thinking that other people must, feeling there had to be a way to represent it. It couldn't just disappear into history without leaving its mark. I was always like that. Everything new or extreme that I felt I needed to do something with.

I got suicidal at times. At a subconscious level I knew I wasn't going to go all the way but I wanted to feel the hurt. There was a thrill about knowing I could cause myself to feel something. It got into this control thing where I just wanted power over myself. I used to keep cutting myself, seeing how far I'd actually go before I would stop. But I would always stop. That's the point: I would always stop.

I somehow knew I was meant to go through all the stuff I had gone through. There is a reason for why I am the way I am. I was meant to live. I'm supposed to do something with this. No matter how much I was being crapped on, and no matter how bad I felt about myself — I always hated myself and thought I was such a *loser* — really, really deep down I *knew* I was meant for something.

At the end of grade seven, I knew I only had one more year at that lousy school. But in the first week of grade eight I got called into the library for a meeting and the principal gave me the choice of going straight to grade nine. I think, aside from knowing I was bright, he was trying to help me get out of that hellhole.

So I started high school when I was thirteen, going on fourteen. That school was interesting but I was only there until the middle of grade ten because we moved again — just as I had started getting used to things. I had finally started making friends in a normal way, and I wasn't such an oddball anymore. I was growing my hair out and getting back in touch with my feminine side, wearing a bit of makeup, looking at boys, and getting influenced by the whole popularity-contest thing.

The new school was totally superficial. I know all high schools are, but this one was obsessed with who was popular and who wasn't. At this school, if you weren't black you didn't have soul. You were just white and you didn't have anything to offer. I don't know how I did it but I guess I got some soul or something. We'd have dances and I'd start busting my moves and people started to see that I did have some soul.

I got respect from some cool people who didn't just want to beat me up. I got accepted and grew a thicker skin. There was fighting all the time in that school. Girls would be getting their hair ripped out in the hallways but I somehow managed to stay away from it and decided that it wasn't going to be part of my life anymore. I had to scheme and strategize about who I needed to become friends with in order to get respect from others. I guess my intelligence saved me. Strategy saved my ass.

Just I was getting in with them, we had to move again. This time it wasn't such a tough school, and there I

was, with such a front now, such a guarded person. I showed up with such attitude because I didn't care anymore. I was so used to being the new kid, the tough kid. I had been through so much that, at that point, nothing could touch me. I guess because of the attitude, people suddenly flocked to me. Everybody wanted to be my friend. That was another trip. Everything at school was finally fine.

During the summers I played a lot of tennis with my dad. He was my tennis coach and I joined a league. It helped me feel like I wasn't such a loser and brought out the competitive side of me. I was nine years old when I started playing tennis, and I joined the league when I was thirteen. It helped balance things out a bit, especially with the transition into high school and finding somewhere to start feeling good about myself.

One thing that saved me is that I was always resourceful and I went after something if I really wanted it. I went back to Hungary to visit when I was eleven years old, and I was so excited to get away for three whole months and be with my grandma. But while I was there, my mom called and said I'd have to go visit my other grandmother for at least a week. I didn't like her because she was fake. I could see my mother in her; they were like clones of each other. She was like a spider or something. When she would talk her phony talk it would make my skin just crawl.

The first two nights of this week-long visit, I cried myself to sleep. I just counted the minutes on my clock. I hated being there, I hated being forced to go for walks, I hated everything I had to do there. About the third day, I went for a walk by myself. I went to the bus station and found out when the next bus was leaving for a nearby town where I had cousins. I called my cousin there and he

agreed to pick me up at the bus station. So I went and bought a ticket. Then I went back to my grandmother's and told her I had to leave earlier than planned because I really wanted to see my sick aunt before I had to go back to Canada.

She looked at me like I was nuts and immediately called my other grandmother on the phone. She laced into my other grandmother, then handed me the phone. I explained to her that I just couldn't stay there anymore.

On the day I was to catch my bus, my grandmother walked me to the bus station in total silence. She didn't say one word. She put my suitcases in front of the bus and just looked at me. I thanked her and said goodbye, and she forced out a goodbye and left me there.

I love that story. I was only eleven years old, but I had a goal and I was resourceful. I did it! This was in Hungary too, and things aren't as easy there. The point of the story is just that, having experienced so much, I know what I don't like.

Looking Back

What advice would I give to other kids who are living through a crazy existence? No matter what you think is happening at any moment, no matter how insane and intense it seems, you can't forget that it is just a moment. After that, there's going to be another moment and it will have something different in it. So to do anything drastic, because of one given moment, is not the answer.

You are the only person who is going to hold yourself back from anything you want in your own life. So if people say you are the ultimate loser, without friends, a geek, then thank all those people. Say, "Thank you! I'm just so thankful that you are telling me all these things because you're right! I'm not like you. I'm me." Just

because they are telling you all these things doesn't mean you have to believe it.

Even though it may seem like the end of the world and there's no way things can get better, just keep pushing yourself. As long as you know what's in your own head and you focus on yourself — on what you want, what you feel, what your instinct says — you'll come through.

I think the turning point for me was a combination of being accepted by my peers, my mother getting a bit better as I got older, and just me. My first experience of being alive was my life with my grandmother. She introduced the world to me as a beautiful place and told me to take all the love into my heart and go out in the world and explore it. She left the seed of love in my heart, the idea that life was great, and I was great, and other people were great, and that I should explore it all. Even though things were rocky for me for a long time, I think the seed from my grandmother was there within me all along. It didn't allow me to totally stop caring.

Not everybody has my grandmother's kind of love given to them. But it's a love for yourself, ultimately, that will get you through. So no matter what's going on, if you really do have respect for yourself, the natural drive will be there. If you stay in touch with it, it will get you through anything.

Maria

Maria was twelve when her father died of AIDS. That event marked the beginning of a difficult time in her life. Her cousins turned on her family, she publicly acknowledged her homosexuality, she thought about suicide, and she dropped out of school. Through it all, she relied on friends who listened and didn't tell her that everything was going to be okay. Her open relations with her brother and mother gave her the strength to see the "light" at the end.

Dad is Dying

I found out my father had AIDS when I was eleven. I had always known he was sick, but until then I never knew what he had.

I had a very cool upbringing. I'm a traditional Italian, but I grew up in a very open-minded household, where we used to sit in the kitchen and have meetings. Nothing was ever hidden from my older brother and me, except the fact that my father was HIV-positive. My brother, who is five years older than me, knew before I did. My mother told me one day when I was in sixth grade. I was getting ready for school. It was getting a bit risky at this stage of the disease, so my mom had to warn me to be careful. She told me to use my own soap and washcloth. I asked why, and she said she'd tell me later, in a year. I said that maybe I didn't have a year, that you never know what's around the corner. She tried to put me off by saying that I was on my way to school, but I said, "So what if I don't get to school? I think you should tell me

now." So she told me: "Your father is HIV-positive."

Although I understood, nothing registered. I didn't even say, "Oh my God!" I think I was in shock. I went to school, and that's where it hit me that my father was going to die. I wasn't afraid of catching it; I never cared about that. I just wanted to spend as much time as possible with him, whatever time that was left, with him and with our family.

We were very close. My parents were never afraid to talk to us, about sex, about drugs. They were very open. I was comfortable going to my father and asking him about periods, about having sex, about men and women, and how they have babies. He was never embarrassed. He was totally cool about everything. If he didn't know something, he would say, "Ask your mother, I think she knows about that better than I do." But he would try to tell me as much as he could. The same was true for my brother. He would go to my mom and ask how to put on a condom, and she'd tell him how to do it. My dad told us he didn't really know how he had contracted the disease. He'd had it for more than twenty years, and he thought it may have happened when he was in the army and they had to share needles for vaccinations.

A Crazy Family

When his disease started getting worse, tension started to build within our extended family. My parents had always shied away from them, preferring an open-minded household where nothing was hidden from the children. But my aunts and uncles were more close-minded. I don't think they could deal with the fact that we were so open. They felt it was silly. They even felt my dad should have told his brothers and sisters about his disease first, before his wife and children. My dad responded that he didn't marry them, or have kids with them. So, when they found out, it was hard for them to accept it. I don't think my father ever accepted it himself. His brothers and sisters began to invite him over to their houses more often, trying to butter him up, because of his will. A lot of tension developed because of the money. They made their interest in that very clear. They made him sign papers saying my brother's and my money had to go to them first, and then they would give it to us. They didn't want my mom to have any money, or control of anything. They even tried to brainwash us, saying that our mother was trying to kill our father, that she was purposely denying him his I.V.

I believed my mom over them. I never doubted her. I knew my own family, but I knew nothing about our extended family. They were very quiet. You know what they say about not being afraid of the dogs that bark: it's the ones that don't bark you should watch out for, because you never know what they're going to do.

I remember the day my father died. We had a meeting at the hospital. My aunts and uncles don't speak English, so they were using my brother as a translator, from the doctors, to them, then to my mom, who speaks English fluently. My uncles were trying to get my brother to tell the doctors that my mother wanted to kill my father, that she was insane and shouldn't be in control. They wanted to be in control of him.

My brother thought they were crazy. He thought they were the ones trying to kill the bond our small family had created. They were threatened by our closeness, and focused on the money. But in the end they didn't get any.

Losing Dad

I was never afraid of touching my father when he was ill. It never crossed my mind. He stayed at home until

Christmas, and he died the following March. You could tell by then that he was very sick. He lost a lot of weight within six months. I did get time with him, and I got to help him too. For one thing, he couldn't sleep in a bed for too long. He liked to change where he slept, so he'd stay in the living room sometimes. We had mattresses on the floor, or sometimes he would sleep on the couch. I started to sleep in the living room with him. I had my alarm clock there, so I could get up and go to school. We had a great relationship.

I had to play the role of nurse with my dad, because my mom had to become both mother and father, and she had to work two jobs. My brother didn't want to deal with it; he'd just take off after school, and he wouldn't come home until bedtime, whereas I would come home and take care of my dad. At one point, he was taking more than twenty pills a day, and I knew exactly which pills to give him at which times. My dad was cooking, though, because he ate different foods, things that I think gave him protein. For a long time I lived on microwave dinners, because my mother was so busy, and the only thing I knew how to cook was fried eggs.

He died a couple of months before my thirteenth birthday. It was hard, because I wanted him to be there for that. For a long time, I was very angry, at him or at some-thing, angry about the fact that he wasn't there for my thirteenth. This was a wish I had made, and at twelve you still think wishes are supposed to come true. There was money under my pillow for my tooth, but my father could-n't be here for my birthday. But I felt that the way my father died was meant to be. We were in the room with him. Although he had started out with his family of birth, he'd spent a lot of his life with his wife and children, so it seemed fitting that we were in the room with him when he

died. His family hadn't accepted his illness and hadn't cooperated on anything; I think he might even have held on, feeling they didn't deserve to be there while he said goodbye to the three of us. He died just half an hour after they left.

After a while, I realized it was better that he had died, because he wasn't in pain anymore. There was a point where he hadn't even recognized us. It's very hurtful for your own father not to recognize you.

My parents were married for twenty years. In all that time, you would think you would come to know your extended family, but my mother said that they had totally blown her away, that she really didn't know them at all. Three years after my father passed away, I visited them, and they started in again, asking if I wanted to know how much money my mom had collected from the insurance company, and commenting on the car she had bought. I know how much money my mom got. I knew she had a car, and where the money came from. So I responded by asking if they knew my father left us with a $25,000 debt. They told me to come to them if I needed anything, but they were still only talking about money. They never asked if my mom had bread on the table, or if our bills were paid. So I don't talk to them anymore. It was too hard for me to talk to people who were trying to pull me away from my own family, from my own mother. I wished they would just stop it.

Facing Homophobia

When I first found out my dad was HIV-positive, I didn't tell anyone; I said he was dying of cancer. So for a long time I wondered if maybe I was ashamed. But I think it was only because of people's attitudes at the time. It was the early nineties, and everyone believed that people who died

of HIV or AIDS were homosexuals. I think many people also believed that if your father was gay, then you would be a lesbian, or your brother would be gay.

So I faced a lot of homophobia once people knew the truth about my father's illness. I would tell someone how he died, and then see them slowly make their way across the room, away from me, though they'd been right beside me minutes before. People assumed that I must have AIDS, or HIV, if my father did. Even his family wanted to get an autopsy done. They still didn't believe it. I felt that this was their issue and they should deal with it, without bringing us into it. We were comfortable with the truth.

"I Know What You're Going Through"

People tried to be supportive of me. But the worst thing to hear, the thing you should never say to someone who is losing someone, is "I know what you're going through." Every time someone said that to me, I would block them out. I'd tell them I couldn't speak to them because they didn't know. Sure, there were things I was going through that people could see, but there was also what was going on inside of me, which no one could see.

There wasn't really anybody to talk to, outside of home. There were teachers I tried to talk to, but I didn't want to tell them something they might not be open-minded enough to handle. I was very close to my cat, Tiger. I had strong ties with friends, but I only hung out with them at school. After school was reserved for being with my dad. There were times when I didn't want to go home, though, because I was afraid of what might happen. There was one incident when my father was worried about my brother; he hadn't called all day and it was late and my mother was at work. I tried to reassure my dad, and said I would call him, but first I had to get my dad his pills.

When I came back with the pills, my father was uncon-
scious and he wasn't breathing. I had to give him mouth-
to-mouth resuscitation, at eleven years old. After I revived
him, he wanted me to rub his heart; he said it hurt. I
wanted to call an ambulance but he didn't want to go to
the hospital. At that point, he'd never gone into the hospital, and he said he wanted to die at home. So I didn't call an
ambulance, but I did tell my mom. When she came home, I
told her she had to do something: either speak to her son
or quit one of her jobs because I'd just had the most frightening experience of my life. So my mom spoke to my
brother.

Feeling Like Dying

I never complained that my dad's illness was more than I
could handle. It was only after he died that I thought that.
And it was only then that I wanted to commit suicide. But
I would catch myself and think, What are you doing,
Maria? You shouldn't be doing this. I didn't hurt myself or
anything, but there were times when I thought of throwing myself off the bridge near my house. I even went to
the bridge, and decided I was going to do it. I was so
angry, and I didn't want to deal with it. For one thing,
there had been all this closeness in my family, and then,
with the difficulties with our relatives, I'd lost the image I'd
had of us as such a good family. My mom was working and
was always tired. My brother was just quiet. I could feel a
lot of negative energy coming from him. So I decided that I
just wanted to be with my dad. But something always
stopped me from killing myself. I would tell myself that I
had my mother and my brother, and that was all I should
need. I decided that I needed to work with them on
regaining the closeness we had all had.

I never told my mom I wanted to kill myself. I had a

social worker through the hospital, but I didn't tell her because I knew she'd tell my mom. I didn't want my mom to have to deal with that. I didn't tell any friends. It was all just between me, my journal and my cat. I would write all the time that I wanted to be with my dad and the only way I knew how to do that was to leave.

A Father Figure

My brother is very different from me. I voice whatever I'm feeling, as soon as I'm feeling it. At most, give me a couple of hours. My brother, though, is very quiet. He doesn't say what he's feeling. So when he does say something, it really has an impact. You think, "Oh, he spoke!" He loved my father a lot, but he was quiet about it, so you never knew how he really felt. Then once, about a year ago, I used his computer, and I saw he had made a diploma, with a picture of my father, saying "Number One Dad." I hadn't known that he felt like that. For a long time I'd even thought he was upset with my father, for reasons I didn't know about. There was some tension, and he didn't want to get too close to him when he was sick.

A memory I have of the day my father died is of my brother walking out of the meeting with my aunts and uncles because he didn't want anything to do with it. I left too and found my brother reading to my father. It was exciting, and moving, to see him reading to my dad, because I had thought he was upset with him. But he wasn't. He was just shielding himself because he didn't want to get hurt. Now my brother and I are much closer than we were when I was younger, say between ten and thirteen, when there used to be a lot of fighting and yelling. That was mostly because I wanted his attention, and he was very quiet. I think he was the next male role model for me, a second father. So we'd get into a lot of

arguments, and we'd say things we didn't mean. At one point, I think I was thirteen or fourteen, I wrote him a letter and apologized for all the things I'd said or done to upset him. I told him it was because I was looking for someone to fill a role that could never be replaced: "You're my older brother, but you're also like a father figure to me now." I stuck the note on his TV. When he saw it, he came into my room, crying. He said, "That's what I wanted to say all along." Now, we have a really close bond. The three of us are living together, and we're close again. We still have our family meetings in the middle of the kitchen.

Coming Out

Grade nine was hard, not just because of my father, but because of personal issues. I was fourteen. I worked after school, at the drug store, as a disc jockey, wherever some-one would pay me. I had to work because we had a $25,000 debt to pay off. Our house was paid for, but we had taken out a second mortgage on it. I took on part of the responsibility because my mother was working three jobs, and she was drained, physically and emotionally. So I told her to stop worrying, to just stick to her full-time job and give up her part-time jobs, that my brother and I would work. And we did.

It was a hard time. I was also dealing with my sexu-ality. I know people think that because my dad had AIDS he must have been gay. And I thought people would think: Your father was gay, that's why you're a lesbian. It was tough to tell my mother about my sexuality. It was within a year of my father's death. I was dealing with my stuff, with my sexual identity, with who I really was and whether I wanted to hide it any longer. I thought, I've put it aside for so long, Dad. Now I have to deal with it. When I told my mom, she was the best. She said, "Well, I still

love you anyway." She said it was fine, that as long as I was happy, she was happy. She was pretty amazing. And my brother said the same thing. I had been having relationships with women, but they were very closeted. Even when my father was dying, I had been in a relationship with another girl. I never told him. I have asked my mom whether she thought my dad would have responded the way she did, and she said she thought he probably would have, that though he might have wanted to walk me down the aisle, he would have wanted my happiness first. As long as I was safe, she said, that was all he'd really care about. Sometimes I wish I could tell my father, but what is meant to be, is meant to be. I think things happen for a reason.

My extended family, aside from my cousins, is not aware of my sexual orientation. I could tell them, but, though I honestly don't care how they respond, I think they would assume I became a lesbian because my dad was gone and my mother couldn't take proper care of me. They would probably think I'd be different if I was living under their roof. But I'm fine. My homosexuality is not because of my mom.

Facing Angry Feelings

After my dad died, I'd go to school, then come home to an empty house. I'd microwave a dinner and do my homework. But then I started rebelling. I was very angry as a thirteen- and fourteen-year-old. I was angry that my father wasn't there and that my extended family had betrayed us. I was being very confrontational and yelling at everyone all the time. I wasn't hearing anybody then. I would say whatever I wanted to say, and then I'd just tune out what anyone else said. You could easily see what an angry person I was. It showed on my face. I even felt tired

of being angry; my face felt tired of being angry.

A year or two after my father died, I got angry at my mother because she was dating. I felt so betrayed. I couldn't stand the thought of her bringing in a replacement for him. The anger broke when my mother confronted me, and I physically pushed her away. I had crossed a line: she was still my parent and deserved my respect. She came right back at me with all this force, saying, "If you're going to push me, I'm going to teach you a lesson. I'll go to jail if I have to, but you'll learn your lesson." I broke down as soon as she put her hands on me. I had reached the point where I had to stop. I was getting into fights at school, over the most minor things, mostly with boys; I wanted them to know they weren't necessarily stronger than me just because they were male. I hated traditional thinking; I wanted to make things equal. I was yelling at teachers. They'd ask what was wrong, and I'd just say that I was really angry. They sent me to a social worker once a week. But that didn't really help because I didn't want to talk about things. At that point, I didn't want to be helped. But when I pushed my mom, I was really disappointed in myself for breaking the bond we had, for crossing a line. That bond was important to me, and that was when I realized I had to get help, that I actually wanted help. I didn't want to lose the only parent I had. I knew I needed to treasure her, not lose her and regret it twenty years later.

That moment of confrontation with my mom was an important moment for the two of us. Some traditions dictate that you hit your kids if you feel they need to be hit, but we weren't brought up that way. We were never yelled at, because that's just noise and children won't listen to noise. You have to speak to them. Hitting was just inflicting pain; kids won't learn anything but pain. So when my mom and I fought that day, that was just pain.

She wasn't listening; I wasn't listening. And we both realized that wasn't the way we'd always strived to be. When I finally broke down, I was able to tell her how angry I was. We had been communicating a bit, but I was leaving things out. She knew about my sexuality at that point, but there were other things I didn't want to deal with, especially the fact that my father wasn't there. For the longest time, I convinced myself that he was away on vacation. I'd think, why is everyone so uptight? Relax! He's coming back.

After the confrontation, I told my mom I was going to get help from the school. I acknowledged that I had been disrespectful to her and that I was ashamed of it. The fact that I had placed my hands on my mother, the one who had taken care of us during this horrible time when we needed her, showed that I didn't appreciate her. So I said I'd get help. She responded, "Good. Go!"

I joined an anger management program at my school. It was good for me, though a lot of the other kids didn't want to be there. They didn't want help, and didn't see that they needed it. I knew I wanted it, so I was there every time I needed to be, doing everything I needed to do. When I finished it, they gave me a little diploma. The program actually helped me; it didn't happen overnight, but it gradually started to show. My family noticed. I stopped yelling.

Leaving School

I left high school in grade ten, to work. I didn't want my mom to have to buy me things like clothes or school supplies. I wanted her to just work toward paying the bills. I wanted to work and give her whatever money she needed. I didn't want our house to be sold. I wanted to keep it, because that was where I'd grown up and where all the happy stuff had happened.

My mom was okay with me leaving school and working. She had always said that whatever I did that was good would benefit me, and that whatever I did that was bad would be bad for me; that it had nothing to do with her and wouldn't affect her; that I needed to think about myself. So when I told her what I was doing, she was okay with it, though at the same time she didn't want me to leave school because of our financial situation. I told her I could always go back, and that if I didn't, she shouldn't worry about it, because it was my choice and it would affect me. So she said okay.

She was happy when I went back to school a couple of years later. I got excellent marks too. I went back partly because I wanted to improve the marks on my record; my previous marks weren't very good because I hadn't been concentrating on school then. There was too much going on. So I wanted to change my barely-passing marks, and I've slowly been able to do that. It's going well so far. This is my last year of school.

I have a couple of different career plans. I want to work in media, maybe television broadcasting. I've already been involved in the industry. I worked for a community TV station, so I have some connections. But right now I'm working in sales, and I want to see how that goes. In TV, you can be at the top one day and you're nobody the next day. In sales, though, it seems more secure. I can always go back to media, because I have some experience. I'll just do this for a year or two, though. I'm young.

Looking Back

If you know someone going through hard times like I did, just listen to them. That's what I needed. I didn't want to hear someone say, "I know what you're going through."

Looking back, I feel that I've lived the lives of five

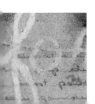

people already. My advice to other kids who may experience a similar situation is, never give up! You hear that all the time, and it sounds corny, but it's true. Keep in mind that things get better, even though you sometimes think it can only get worse

There's always the light. It's so hard to see that when you're going through stuff. I thought I was really alone, but now I've heard so many people talking about all the hard things in their lives, and how then they discovered the light. So just keep fighting for that light. For sure, the light will be there.

Randy

Randy barely remembers a time when his parents were together. He has never had a father figure to look up to. In order to cope with memories of being sexually abused and being picked on at school, Randy turned into a tough kid who wouldn't let anyone get close to him. He dealt with his problems by acting out, running away, and taking drugs. Saved by a friend, who locked him away in his room to get the drugs out of his system, he finally started rebuilding his life. His advice to other kids: Don't run away from your problems. They'll only come back to haunt you.

Looking for Trouble

My mom got divorced from my dad when I was five, and after that she and my sister and I moved around a lot. We lived in suburban areas, in apartment buildings, where my mom was always dodging the rent payments and lying to the landlords. My issues started at eleven or twelve years old. I was a pretty good kid until then.

My mom raised me to love everybody equally. That's one of the things I like about her. She's pretty amazing. She's a former hippie, from Ireland. It's hard when she gets mad at you: her accent gets stronger and she talks faster so you can't understand what she's saying. You have to try not to laugh.

Because we moved so much, I met a lot of people. I got to know a lot of troublemakers in Boston, where I lived. They say kids get into trouble because they're looking for attention. It wasn't really about that for me. It was just something to do. My mom worked, so I would pick up my sister from school, take her home and make dinner, and basically take care of her until my mom came home from work at nine o'clock.

At age thirteen the really bad stuff started. I began getting into a lot of trouble. At first it was small stuff, like shoplifting. I was hanging out with a group of people like me, losers in school that nobody liked. We didn't like anybody else either. We acted out our aggression on people we didn't know by stealing from stores and stuff. That's also when I started smoking weed, and when I had my first sexual experiences. That was interesting.

Stand-ins for Dad

My mom had a lot of boyfriends who were alcoholics. I think she was with them to use their money to support us, more than because she really cared about them. But it was confusing for me, my mom dating all those trashy guys. They probably had a hand in starting my troubles too. Either they came in with the attitude that they weren't my dad, they were my buddy, or they acted like they *were* my dad and they could tell me what to do because they were dating my mom. I wouldn't stand for either one. They made me sick, or pissed off, or both.

The first guy she dated was a truck driver who weighed about 290 pounds. He was a cranky guy who worked nights and slept days, which gave me ample opportunity to steal his keys, unlock his truck and take his money. I stole from him a lot. When he noticed and told my mom, she would act like I was this angel. On one occasion, though, Mom talked to me about it, saying she knew I had taken his money. After she basically interrogated me, I admitted it and showed her where the money was. She thought where I'd hidden it was quite clever. He never saw the money. She kept it.

He wasn't physically abusive but I think I would have preferred that, because a lot of the stuff he used to say had an effect on me for a long time afterward. Stuff like that has an emotional impact and you carry it with you at some level. You might not consciously think those negative things about yourself, but somewhere in your head you remember them. Then they're amplified by the fact that you're getting beaten up and picked on at school, called a little geek and a loser, getting your face stepped on. It just doesn't have a positive effect on your life.

I had this girlfriend who helped me torture him. Once we took maple syrup, eggs, dog doo, kitty litter, anything you can think of, and piled it all under the sheets in his bed. That night I was upstairs in my room on the third floor, waiting, when he came home and went to bed. All I heard was cussing and swearing. I was scared to death but I was giggling like a schoolgirl. He knew it was me, but my mom wouldn't let him come near me. Shortly after that he moved out.

My mom's next boyfriend drank a lot, and he was one of the "I'm your buddy, not your dad" kind of guys. At first he tried hard; I've got to give him that. He tried to be my buddy, but only when he drank, and he drank a lot. He used to make up stories about how he had been robbed, to make himself look like this big, tough guy, but it was just drunken babbling that you knew wasn't true.

He began to behave really badly toward my mom and me. Then he raped my sister. She told me not to tell anybody, so I just hinted around to my mom to see if she knew anything. Although she knew that something had happened, she didn't know it was rape. A week or two later it almost happened again, and my mom actually walked in on it. That was when she called the cops. I guess she didn't really believe it when I told her, because she

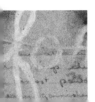

knew I hated him. I guess she figured it was just a way for me to get back at him and I was just dragging my sister into it with me. But eventually she knew I was right.

Now my mom's with a great guy. I didn't like him when I first met him but he's made a better impression, bit by bit. I like him because he's not a drinker, he works for the City, and he's got my mom working there part-time too. He's pretty smart; he's got street smarts. When I first met him he said something that just rubbed me the wrong way and I turned around and said, "You don't even know who the hell I am! You're talking like you've known me my whole life." He stood up and looked at me, then he basically cut me down to size and totally deflated my ego. He was saying stuff about how I was full of myself and how I should drop the tough-guy act. I was really pissed off — because he was right. That's why I didn't like him, but I guess that's what ended up impressing me the most. After that, we started to level with each other. He's been around for three years now. He's a pretty straight-ahead guy, and he's really good to my mom.

The Bad Kid

I didn't really have time for myself as a kid and that really frustrated me. It was expected that I would take care of my sister a lot. I felt like I was doing things that I shouldn't and that weren't really my responsibility, things that a babysitter should do. I took her to school in the morning, picked her up at lunchtime, took her home and made her lunch.

We used to have babysitters, but there was some sexual abuse that happened when we were young, so my mom didn't trust sitters anymore. That's not something I can really talk about, because I'm not sure about it. I have two flashes of memory about it, that's all. I know something took place, but I don't know exactly what. I'd like to know; I don't like not being sure of my own memories. It's really confusing. But I know it resulted in my mom not trusting babysitters and my having to take care of my sister. She and I were pretty close, until she started going to another school and I started getting in trouble, hanging out with my friends and thinking I was too cool for anybody. We started drifting apart after that.

At school, kids always targeted me, because I was mouthy. We weren't very well off, so I wore a lot of recycled clothing, and that always makes you a great target for other kids. I didn't care because at least I had clothes. I feel really bad when I think about it now because my mom went through a lot to help look after my sister and me.

In junior high I had a lot of problems at school and I got into a lot of trouble. I was telling teachers where to go. By then I had the idea that bad kids were cool. I'd seen too many movies where everybody thought that. Everyone was scared of the bad kids, but they liked them at the same time. They got all the girls. It kind of did work out that way in my life. And I acted like the bad kid at school because that was better than being the one who got beaten up all the time. It was sort of a protection for me.

Dad Shows Up

I didn't know my dad. He got out of paying child support by working part-time. All I had to go on were stories my mom and my grandmother used to tell me about him. I had never seen him. I talked to him once when I was eight and once when I was thirteen, but nothing substantial. I only knew a bit about him. He would call during the summer when I was at my grandmother's, and he'd say six sentences, and that was that.

I think that's a big part of the reason I kept getting in

trouble. I didn't really have a father figure around to repri-
mand me, or to kick me through a wall if that's what I
needed. Not that I think that's right. But I didn't have a
disciplinarian.

I heard that my dad had married a woman with a
daughter named Linda. It turned out that we had gone to
school together, but we'd had no idea we were going to be
each other's new brother or sister. It's funny the way it all
happened. Linda came up to me and said: "I didn't know
John Adamson was your dad. He's the guy who's dating
my mom."

I called her one day, and my dad answered. Of
course, I didn't recognize his voice. Linda wasn't home so
he said he'd take a message. I told him it was Randy, and
there was a full minute of silence. It seemed like five minutes. Finally he asked if I knew who he was. I said no, and
he told me that he was John Adamson and he was my
father. It just blew me away.

He ended up coming to pick me up, saying they
would give me a place to stay and that we would work
something out. That's when I found out about his new
marriage and his whole new family. I figured that was why
he hadn't kept his old responsibility: he'd just gone out
and gotten a new one! I got in trouble there too, because it
was hard seeing him with a new family. I started stealing
from other people in the house and I started telling off my
stepmother.

Ups and Downs

About a year later, when I was almost fifteen, I think, I
met the best girlfriend I've had in my life: Maria.
Everybody has that one best girlfriend, but I was a bad
kid with a sad life and no one to talk to, and she really
was a great thing that happened to me. She used to hang

out with our next-door neighbor and another girl our age. She was so pretty. I would see her at the lake we swam at. My friends and I would push her in the water and make her laugh. We came up with the nickname Miss Giggles because she always laughed at everything I said.

My whole world changed after I met Maria; my life started revolving around her. I'd go to school, but if she was sick I'd skip off and stay with her, take care of her, make soup for her. I was a really sweet guy to her. She was the first person in my life that I actually talked to. I stopped getting in trouble for a while.

After three years, Maria and I broke up because I cheated on her. Well, I didn't actually cheat on her; I kissed another girl. That was a big thing then. But it wasn't just that, it was the breach of trust. After being with somebody for three years, you just don't do that, even if it's only one kiss.

Because we'd been together for so long, and I was a nice guy, she was willing to look past it and keep things going. I really wanted to buy her a promise ring then. That's like an engagement ring. I did get her a ring, but the way I got it wasn't so great.

I'm not proud of the things I'm telling you, especially this. It's my biggest shame.

We used to visit New Handsford every summer for two weeks, so I took Maria on vacation with my mom and me. We had a great time. We had a lot of friends at home, but some of them had been telling her to break up with me. We were already trying to overcome this whole crack in the foundation of trust, and we didn't need this squabbling going on around us. So it was great, the two of us in the country together. But before we left at the end of the holiday, I stole a $1,500 check from my grandmother.

When we got back to Boston, I got Maria's mom to

cash it on her account, with the excuse that it was money that my grandmother gave me every year to buy school clothes. My grandparents figured it out, though, and it's never been the same with them since then. They used to be so generous; they sent me so many presents at Christmas and on my birthday. After that, nothing. I didn't talk to them for several years. I would have loved to be able to work up the guts to apologize to them.

After the check incident, my dad and stepmother got close to my grandmother, because she called and talked to them about it. If I could, I'd return the $1,500 to them and apologize. Then I'd feel a lot better. My mom kept saying that it's not the money they cared about. I did apologize to them over the phone, but that's impersonal. I'm more of a face-to-face person. I just wish I could have evened out what I did.

I finally went out there last summer, but I was too ashamed to say anything to my grandmother about the check. She and my grandfather just acted like nothing had happened. But I could tell they were thinking about it and wondering what I was up to. I was so glad that I hadn't just put off going to see her, like I'd always done before, because she died shortly after that visit.

My dad kicked me out after I stole the check, and Maria broke up with me. Everything went downhill after the check. There I was, trying to show this girl that I was someone who she could trust and depend on and my life was going downhill. It hurt more that Maria broke up with me than my dad kicking me out.

Living on the Street

I couldn't go anyplace around Boston without thinking about how many places I had been with Maria and how many memories we had shared. It brought me really low,

and so did the place I was living and the people I was living with then. I wasn't in school; I wasn't doing anything. I was just sitting in a welfare house, living off other people, not even energetic enough to go get welfare for myself.

So when a friend came by, I decided to just split with him. We hitchhiked for three days, and I ended up in Chicago. I didn't want to get a job; I didn't want to go anywhere in life. I just wanted to party. I didn't have any money. We used to go through the garbage bags at Dunkin' Donuts and take their donuts. I hate donuts now. I can't even look at one without feeling nauseous.

In Chicago I found a squat to sleep in. Then I started doing PCP. I had a really bad problem with that. I got addicted to it, though it was hard for people to see that.

At first, I was panhandling a bit and scamming people, because I was pretty good at talking. But I didn't like it because I wasn't really doing anything but sitting on my butt, looking like a bum. So I started squeegeeing. It was tough at first because there were a lot of turf wars, and you had to be known: If you just walked up to a corner with a squeegee without knowing anybody you got chased off. Or you'd be allowed to work there for an hour or so, but you wouldn't go home with any money or your squeegee.

But I liked moving around and working up a sweat some days to make my money. It was great money. Some guys were nice and would give you a five-dollar bill, and others would even flip you a twenty. This guy in a Porsche gave me a hundred-dollar bill once. That was the best.

I used it to buy eight caps of PCP. That's where a lot of my money went. Taking PCP was always like a new beginning: it made me feel like I could be someone better, not a little geek everyone beats up. It made me feel like I wasn't going to take shit from anybody. I was just going to

be me, and do what I wanted to do, when I wanted to do it.

Eventually I moved out of the squat and booked into the Y House because I caught scabies. That is the nastiest thing about the street. I'd rather take people spitting on me and insulting me than ever get scabies again. It's horrible. And sometimes the treatment doesn't work: you miss one spot and you're screwed. I had to leave the squat because the place was infested. My clothes got infested and so did I. I had to get everything cleaned, and I had to do the treatment three times. I got over scabies, but I was still doing PCP.

Kicking the Habit

I ended up getting a place with a new friend, James. People still talk about that place. It became a legend with the street kids. I was still doing PCP then, and I tried to hide it from James, but he knew. He just didn't say anything.

But it was getting really bad, and I knew I had to quit. I told James I wanted to quit and asked for his help. He told me I'd probably consider his help more of a punishment after a few days, and I might not want it anymore. He warned me pretty well. Then he came back with a bottle of water and told me I couldn't leave the room for three days. He wouldn't let me out for anything; he even had me escorted to the bathroom. I didn't realize how badly addicted I was, physically, until he did that.

During my three days in my room, all I had was a table, my TV, and a liquor bottle collection I had going because I liked all the shapes and colors. I ended up kicking it out in frustration when I was craving PCP. That was the second day. I was bawling on the couch, and James came in and held me. I'm not used to that. With my past, I'm not comfortable with a guy touching me, but James was there for me the whole time, even though a lot of it is

a blur for me. I guess I was a real asshole. At one point, we got into a fistfight in the bedroom. But he didn't give up on me; he still helped me out. On the third day, he let me out and said I could do whatever I wanted, that that was all he could do for me. He said I could go out and snort a line, but it would be the last time I'd see him, and the last time he'd hang around with me.

I almost went back out that day, but I didn't. It's been almost five years since then. I'm working two jobs now, one at a restaurant and the other at a pizza place, which was the first job I ever got. For a year or two after I quit PCP, I was still squeegeeing, and hanging around with punk rockers who did a lot of the stuff. People would offer it to me and I'd say no. It wasn't that I was so strong. It was because I saw what other people were like on one cap. I could only imagine what I must have been like on three or four or five. The high for me was the invincible, big-man feeling. I would try to start a fight with anybody. You get so aggressive. I mouthed off to anybody because I wasn't scared when I was on it. I had been so used to being afraid of things, and it was a way of escaping fear. I don't do that anymore, but even talking about it now, I still want it. Once an addict, always an addict.

Coming Through the Craziness

Giving advice to a kid who's experiencing things similar to what happened in my childhood is tough, because I ran away from it. But running away doesn't work; it doesn't solve anything. What happened stays in your head and your heart; it will always be with you. It might be over, but in your mind nothing is over with. You can always play it again in your head, and you can always feel it. So running isn't the best thing, but trying to deal with it, with no life experience, is hard too. Just try to bear with it, I guess.

I feel like I've moved on, but a lot of my friends think I'm still stuck in the past on some things: Maria, my grandmother, my mom, my dad. It's true that there are still things I've left unsaid, for so long that it seems almost irrelevant to say them. But they're still important enough to me that I want to say them.

So there's some advice I can give: If you have something to say, say it while you can. You don't know when you may no longer be able to, and you may regret not having said it.

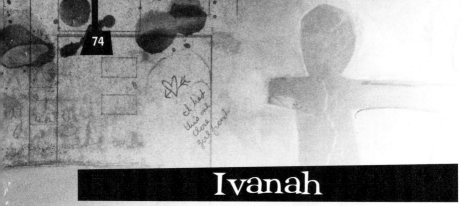

Ivanah

Ivanah was dealing with the problems of being the child of immigrant parents when her mother developed a serious mental illness. Suddenly she had to be the parent her little brother and sister had lost and the supportive partner her father no longer had to lean on. Today she's turning her bad fortune around and has a lot to tell teenagers who are going through similar tough times: hang in there, work hard, and, most important, find someone to talk to about your problems.

Strangers Among Us

I remember a Smurf pin I had when I was six that said "Boys are stronger, but girls are smarter." That particular stereotype stayed with me for a very long time. That was when I began putting distinct labels on the role of everyone in my life and on my role in the world. It stuck with me and had a huge impact on who I became.

My parents were born and raised in Vietnam but received their education in Korea, which is where I was born. We came here when I was about a year old. I guess I'm as American as they come.

The first time things started to get a little nuts in my family was when I was about ten. We had sponsored my cousins' immigration here from Vietnam. They're my mom's sister's kids, the youngest of eight children, and they were twelve and seventeen when they first left Vietnam on a boat for Malaysia, where they lived in a refugee camp for a year or two.

Their arrival here made me feel like my life was very

different from the lives of everyone else I knew. We lived in a small three-bedroom house, and when my cousins moved in that made seven of us, including five kids. They were complete strangers to us, living in our house. That was when things started getting really crazy at home. It launched me into a pretty intense depression; I remember feeling suicidal at ten.

My brother and sister were fine with it; there were just more people for them to play with. But I was older and at a different point in my life. I had to share a room with one of my cousins. Both my parents were working, trying to support seven people instead of five, so there was a lot of sacrifice on their part. For me, the whole house had shifted.

My cousins lived with us for three years. Things had gotten so tense by then, I never knew whether they left or got kicked out. Here were these people who had been living a life with few rules in a refugee camp, and suddenly they were living in a new house, in a different country, with all these rules to follow. One of my cousins was a smoker and couldn't smoke in the house. He was eighteen and wanted his independence. I remember at one point they both wanted to go on welfare, and my mom said they could, but only if they paid rent to her.

At school, I felt totally isolated. I didn't get along with any of the girls. I was an outcast for a long, long time and I never figured out why. They just didn't like me.

It was a really *white* school, with only a couple of minority kids. The school always preached the right theories, and it was liberal and totally cool; I got a great education there, and it played a huge part in the way I look at the world today. But it was weird being one of only three Asian kids, trying to feel comfortable and accepted in that world while everyone around me seemed to have a very different life.

In high school, I never did much socializing until the later years. I didn't have a strong peer group until then. I had friends, but I only saw them occasionally, when I wasn't working, sleeping, eating, volunteering, babysitting, or taking care of my family.

Illness Strikes

My mom went back to school, to college, about the time my cousins moved out. But she got sick when I was fourteen and after that she never went back to work. She has schizophrenia. I think she was originally diagnosed with it at twenty-eight and was in the hospital in Korea for six months. I assume the treatments back then, in 1978, must have been really different. After that first episode, I think she was pretty stable. She came here, had all three of us, and then got sick again right after she had my brother, though I have no recollection of it. I don't know whether she was on medication then, but she is now. We finally found her a really good balance of medication in 1997; it took four years of tinkering. She's been better since then.

Her illness developed kind of gradually. She was working part-time and began to think everybody at work was talking about her. She hated being out in public. She began to hate my father for things she thought he was doing. It got to the point where she told me she couldn't deal with it anymore. She said she kept hearing voices in her head, telling her things. She described it as aliens invading her space and yelling at her to do something, but she could never figure out what that something was.

When my mom got sick this time, I was in Germany on a student exchange. When I came back, I found out she was in the hospital. It was scary. I was in grade nine. My dad said I could never leave the house again because she had gotten sick while I was away. I guess he was half-joking; I think he meant it as a way of saying he needed me for support. But I blamed myself for a long time.

My aunt, who lives in California, is schizophrenic too. She and my mom are on the same medication. I think their schizophrenia must have been triggered by their environment, and by stuff from their childhood. That makes sense to me, but of course I don't really know. My mother's family didn't have anything to do with us while my mom was sick; they don't talk about mental illness.

A Change of Roles

Seeing my mom fall to pieces was really scary. She was supposed to be taking care of me, nurturing me. It was really difficult. I couldn't understand why it was happening, and I couldn't figure out what to say to her. I tried to do this huge role reversal in my head: I knew that if I was sick my mom would try to help me, so I knew I had to help her. I just sat and listened and tried to figure out what to do. But I didn't have any answers.

I had already begun looking after my younger siblings when my mom returned to school, though not as much as I had to after she got sick. I was in sort of a surrogate-parent role. My parents were actually pretty lax in their parenting style. There was very little discipline because we didn't get in much trouble. My sister and I were really hard-working, and my brother was really bright, so they weren't worried about us. There wasn't a real parent in the sense that nobody really put their foot down.

I also became kind of emotionally responsible for my siblings, trying to explain to them that Mom was sick, and what that meant. It's one thing to see a parent physically ill, but mental illness isn't talked about in our society. I might look at the crazy woman on the corner, but to associate that with *my mother* was so difficult. Yet those are

the images that we have of mental illness. So trying to get my brother and sister to understand that our mom was sick in that way was really difficult.

I had to be a big support for my dad too. I don't think he had many friends he could talk to about this. I don't think it's easy for anyone to say that their wife is "going crazy." So I was the person he talked to. In that sense, my dad and I were really close. I remember one morning after a bad night of fighting with my mom, my dad just broke down. He had lost all hope and seemed really depressed. He said he didn't know how to help her, didn't know how to fix it, and didn't even know what he was doing here anymore. I think he was almost suicidal then. I don't think he would ever have abandoned his wife and children — but he was so lost.

Reaching Out

It was really tough. But when I was about sixteen, I was lucky to be dating someone who was really supportive and amazing and wonderful. Having such strong support was one reason I got through it all. The community work I was doing was also really important to me. I didn't have any teachers that I talked to, but a couple of my guidance counselors were there for me. I think it was really key that I had a few good people in my life, youth workers I could call who directed me to places for counseling and support. I wasn't in formal counseling then, though I've been doing that recently. But there were a lot of good people looking out for me back then, which made it easier. And I was always busy. I've worked pretty steadily since I was four-teen, in the summers and part-time through the school year.

So I was living at home, not really able to do much except listen and be a good support for my mother and my

father. And I was trying to keep it together at school and at work, which was a really good distraction. Mostly it was good to be in places where I felt safe and needed. It was important for me to have a handle on things and make things work. That's probably why I worked so hard, and why I continue to do that.

A Turning Point

The breaking point for us came when my mom threw a camcorder at the living room wall and put a hole in it. She and my dad were fighting. Often my mom believed that my father had done things to her, or she would fight with him in her head but think they were actually fighting. My dad loved my mom, so seeing her dream up all this stuff was hurtful and frustrating for him. This time they got into a huge fight. My mom got so angry she picked up a hockey stick and went after my father. Ordinarily, she was the most passive, quiet woman; I'd never seen her get violent before. I was seventeen at the time. I was holding her back, my sister was bawling, and my brother was just stunned. My dad was in tears. He was so lost. He couldn't understand why my mother was doing this. So I sent him out for a walk, telling him that I was just going to calm Mom down and then I'd come and find him.

I told my mom that we couldn't live like this anymore, that Dad hadn't been doing anything wrong, and that I needed her to not behave badly towards him. I said I needed her to be there for me and I needed her to get herself together. I think she knew then that something had to be done.

We ended up making an appointment for her, my dad, and me to see her psychiatrist the next day. It was a turning point: we realized it wasn't just my mom who needed therapy, but that we all needed to figure out how to deal with her disability. For one thing, she wasn't on the right medication yet. It was a couple of months later that we finally found that. What a relief. After that, she began to be more stable and happy. She and my dad started spending some quality time together, and things got so much better.

Losing Dad

That was a few years ago. My mom is doing well now. She's not working, and I don't think she'll go back to work. But she volunteers at the public library, tutoring kids on Thursday afternoons, and she really enjoys it. It's amazing: she called me once to tell me that she had gone to volunteer that day and she'd had fun. It was the first time I'd heard her say she'd had fun. Ever.

So she's been stable for a couple of years. But something very traumatic happened last fall. My father had a stroke and died suddenly. I found out later that he had stopped taking his medication about six weeks before he died. He had high blood pressure and high cholesterol, but he figured that as long as he ate carefully and did his exercises he didn't need the medicine anymore. I felt so angry with him about that.

It happened at home on Thanksgiving weekend. I had stayed at school to study. My mom called me. She and my dad had been getting ready to go out for dim sum and they'd had an argument. She was downstairs when she suddenly heard a boom on the floor. My dad had passed out and he'd stopped breathing.

When I got to the hospital, my dad had just come out of surgery. He was in a coma for three days, and then we lost him. He was forty-nine. It just came out of nowhere. It was really hard.

My mom was amazing. Her life has changed drastically since then. It was their twenty-fifth anniversary the week after he died. We were a bit afraid that she would relapse, and all the craziness would start again. But she has become much stronger. My brother and sister are doing well too. They're eighteen and sixteen now. We still haven't gotten to a point where we can talk about my father, though. There's still a lot of stuff we need to work through, but we're slowly getting there.

One thing my dad's death has meant is that there's no room for me to be slack. I have to be a lot more responsible at home, be the strong person. For a long time that job was split between my dad and me. But it's getting easier because my siblings aren't little kids anymore either.

My brother and I aren't very close right now. I think it has to do with the fact that he's a sixteen-year-old boy and I'm a twenty-year-old girl and we don't have much in common at this point, but we get along. My sister and I get along really well. I probably talk to her once or twice a week, though not as much as I talk to my mom. My sister is wonderful. I think the reason she and my brother are doing so well is that they both have strong peer groups and a lot of people they can talk to. My brother's closest friend also lost her father a year ago. I think it helps to know others who have experienced the same kind of loss; it helps you to realize that, hard as it is, loss is part of life.

My relationship with my mom has changed a lot. It's on an even footing now. She's really wonderful and supportive to me. My family and friends have told me that I have to get myself together and come home. The thought of that absolutely terrifies me. But my mom lets me do my own thing. She's really respectful and responsive.

Leaving home for school had been hard, at first, especially after what had happened with my cousins and

my mom. I felt so guilty for so long, but my dad and I talked about it a lot, about why it was important for me and the good things that would come out of it. My mom and I talked about it too, and we decided that I would go away to school for four or five years, and then I'd come back and everything would be as it was before. It probably won't be that way, though. I don't see myself living in that house after I've finished school.

Looking Back

I think growing up with a mother who suffered from a mental illness made me really respect people and empathize with them. I think realizing that you could lose control to that level, lose all sense of security and stability, taught me that nothing is constant. It made me see that you have to take what you have and be grateful for it, respect and cherish it while you have it, and make it as strong as you can because you don't know when it may disappear.

The relatives I have here in North America live in California and Arizona, but I didn't see them for years. Mental illness is not talked about in Vietnamese culture. My mom went down to visit them for five weeks when I was seventeen. I think it was one of the best things she could have done. She spent time with her sisters, which was great for her, but they weren't a big part of our family's life. They only got reintroduced to us at my dad's funeral. At that time, I didn't appreciate them telling me what to do, when they weren't part of my mom's daily life and I was. It was invasive, but I understood why they were doing it.

I only started talking to my cousin about my aunt's illness after my dad died. His death sort of opened up a Pandora's box of things that had never been talked about before, which I think is a good thing.

Coming Through

My advice to other kids who may be experiencing a similar childhood struggle is, be patient. It gets easier. It takes a lot of awfully hard work and it's really exhausting in a way that I can't even describe. It drains you. At some point you'll hit rock bottom, and it will be dark and awful and gruesome, and you'll be there for a while. But it gets easier. You just have to wait it out and get through it. There are steps to take, and leaps you have to make, and you will. It's just a matter of time.

I really don't believe in bottling things up and denying your experiences. I think it's the main way Vietnamese culture deals with trauma, though. For me, it's not an effective way of getting through things; running from your past and pretending it doesn't exist doesn't make any sense to me. I think a lot of people do it to cope, but I don't think it's helpful in the long run. I'm a big talker. I'm very loquacious. I think that's healthy. It may not work for my siblings or my mom, but it's important for me.

I'm studying political science and women's studies at college now. I'm very happy there. My dream job is to be mayor, because I think the best way to help people is from that spot. A mayor can directly influence public policy: I could find more money for daycare and childcare, things like that.

That's probably something anyone can do: commit to things and work hard at things they care about. Find things to do that make you feel good. I've worked as hard as I have because I love the things I do. I couldn't do it otherwise.

Sajeed

Sajeed was sent away from his Caribbean home when he was seven years old because his parents thought he looked "uncomfortable." In reality, he had been sexually abused by their friends and was acting up to get attention from anyone who would listen. Living in Detroit with his grandparents, he continued to push the limits and break the rules, until he had to flee to Chicago because someone wanted to kill him. He rushed into bad situations and ended up on the street with very few friends. Now Sajeed is finally settling down and holding a job. His advice to kids growing up in tough times: stay calm and take your time.

Far From Home

When I was seven I left the Caribbean, where I lived with my parents and my younger sister, and I went to live in Detroit with my grandparents. I didn't know why I was sent away from my parents. I couldn't understand why they wouldn't want me.

I think they may have thought it would be a good opportunity for me to experience something different. But I believe today that if I had stayed there things would have been a lot easier for me. My education probably would have been much better because the Caribbean educational system is the greatest. You can't make much money down there and people have to strive for luxuries and stuff, but that doesn't mean much to me. I don't think it meant anything to me as a kid either.

At first I thought I would only be living up here for a while. I had no idea it would be for so long. When I

moved here I really didn't like it. I found the change too difficult. The question I always asked myself was, why would they send me here?

Living with my mom's parents was stressful. My aunts and uncles sent their kids to my grandparents' too, so they had a lot of kids in the house. My cousin and I shared a room, and all the girls shared another room, and my uncle was downstairs. My grandparents were sort of parents to all of us, but nobody got what they needed.

My parents sent my sister up here four years after they sent me. I took care of her a lot. My grandparents were churchgoers, and I think they thought I was the bad seed or something; they tried to separate us a lot. But my sister was so loving that she couldn't let go of me. When we'd go to church and I'd have to go to Sunday school, a lot of times she'd follow me to my class. My grandparents never understood how she could be so different from me and yet want to be around me all the time.

I got in a lot of trouble at school at times, but I took care of my sister first. We'd go to school together in the morning, but leaving school at the end of the day was a task because I'd want to stay back and talk to people. Lots of times she wanted to go home before I did, so I left early and took her home. But she also rescued me a lot. If she saw me doing something stupid, she'd come up to me and say, "Let's go home." A lot of times, she'd be behind me and I wouldn't even know until she saved me.

Neither of us was very happy up at my grandparents' without our parents there. We would call our mom down in the Caribbean, and she would end up crying because we were crying. So finally my mom came up here. But there wasn't enough room at my grandparents', so they kicked us all out of their house.

I think my mom understood what we had been going

through because she remembered her teenage years living with her parents. So when she came up here she quickly got a place for us. She has that street mentality. If we couldn't afford food, she'd know to go to the Salvation Army, or she'd go out the next day and get a job. She's a fast thinker.

It only took me a week to settle into my mom's new place, but my sister didn't really like it. I could tell the adjustment wasn't too cool for her. It was winter and she wanted to be back in the Caribbean.

Secrets and Lies

I know one of the reasons my parents sent me up here was because I felt uncomfortable down there with my family. But it wasn't my parents who did anything to me. I was molested by a friend of my parents and a woman. I shouldn't have gone through those experiences. I was just a kid.

I never told my parents about being molested. I hid it from them, but they could tell that I was uncomfortable for some reason. I really tried to tell my dad's mother about what had happened to me. But after I did, she just told my parents that I needed to live somewhere different, I guess. That's when they sent me up here to be with my mom's family.

When I got to Detroit, I told my maternal grand-mother about being molested, but she didn't believe me either. Often, after I'd tried to tell her about things that were on my mind and she wouldn't listen, I'd do something bad just to get punished. I guess I looked for punishments because I wanted someone to care. I wanted someone to understand me, and listen to what I had to say. Most of the time I would try something just to get attention. I'd act really ridiculous. I overreacted a lot. When my grandmother accused me of lying about things, I actually started lying, to try to get her attention, but I never got it.

I actually just told my parents two years ago, for the first time, about what happened in the Caribbean. I don't know how they felt, or whether they were embarrassed. They said I should have told them. I could see that they felt bad, and for some reason that made me feel good. I think it's because I had been waiting for a reaction to it all my life. I guess I just figured they'd find out about it without me having to tell them. I never told them about it before because I thought they'd just react like my grandmother had — saying I was lying and that I wasn't allowed to say such things about people.

Trouble At School

For a long time, I couldn't read a thing. It's gotten better, but from the fifth to ninth grades, when they were trying to teach me to read, it was a problem. In high school, I still wasn't reading very well.

Homework was torture. I was always being told to go and do my homework. But the way I saw it, I had already gone to school that day, so having to bring all this stuff home was even more aggravating. I'd sit and think about the person who kept telling me to do this and do that. I'd bring my work home, but I'd never do it. Sometimes, when they had the time, my grandmother or my aunt or my cousin would come downstairs and spend an hour with me while I did it. They would sit there and show me how to do something, and then I'd do it on my own. Then they'd tell me to try the next question, or to try a question that was a bit harder, and I couldn't do it. Eventually, they'd just give up on me. It was so frustrating. I hated it. It was as if trying to find someone to help me was a full-time job. Getting help from my family felt

like begging, even though I never said a word.

There were some helpful teachers in grade school. Some of them wouldn't try to make me read. They knew I was always distracted, so they wouldn't try to force me.

I remember one teacher, though, who would always play games with me. It was a class for special kids and she'd tell me that she didn't know why I was there because I was a quick thinker. She was so cool. Even though I've left school now, I go back to see this teacher and she's still the same cool lady. I never talked to her about my personal stuff, though.

At high school I got into a lot of trouble. I felt stressed out and really pissed off, but I smiled all the time and never let anybody know. I blew up the school elevator once by playing with matches, trying to impress everybody, and I got suspended. That same day, some people from somewhere else showed up to fight. They even had machetes. The school thought I was part of that and I got in so much trouble. By the time they found out I hadn't been involved, I had already transferred to another school.

Things really went downhill at the new school. The problems I already had seemed a lot worse because I felt so alone there. And being alone was such a big part of the problem in the first place! It was probably the worst time of my life, because I was going through being a teenager. My mom didn't understand, the teachers didn't understand, I didn't understand. The teachers probably go through the same things with their teenage kids, who probably don't understand either.

What I really wanted to have was an older person who would take control. I needed someone to mentor me, but the closest I could get was hanging around with a bunch of guys. We made up a name for ourselves and ran around and did stupid things. I really could have used

someone just to go out and do sort of father-son things with me. I finally found someone like that many years later, but it was too late. I'd gotten into too much trouble by then.

All my friends were out on their own too. I could never actually talk to them about my issues. I knew if I talked about certain things, it would just be a laugh, or that everybody would then know about it. So I grew up always smiling, not letting anybody know how I really felt.

I'm very sociable because I learned as a kid how to make friends really quickly. But as a teen my friendships were sort of on and off. I kept friends at a distance. For instance, if I really liked a girl, I'd probably talk to her every day but she would never know how I really felt. I'd never let her know.

Dad Shows Up

Halfway through high school my father came into the picture. He moved up here from the Caribbean. When he came here, we didn't have a relationship, but I still loved him. It was really weird. His father had not treated him with respect. His father never listened to him, or even talked to him. He was an older man, and he had fourteen kids. He lived on a plantation and didn't work, so he was around to tell my father what to do all the time.

My dad's a very sociable guy, like me. We're similar in that way, but I try to avoid being like him. We never really got along. Even though I might think he was right, we'd argue, just to make a point. We loved each other, you could tell, but we liked to fight. He never understood any-thing about the teenage attitude in Detroit and I never understood what he was trying to tell me about his teenage years. He had had such a strict life and he couldn't do that to me. He didn't want me to go through that. He came here to get an education, even though his father had told him he couldn't come here.

I think my dad's presence in my life really tore me up. I wanted to be closer to him, but there was too much history that we weren't ready to deal with for that to happen. I had so much on my mind that I couldn't tell him, because if I did, it would lead to talking about the sexual abuse and I'm not sure we were ready to go there. I know that. I just kept lying to everybody about things because they had never believed me when I told the truth. I lied about really ridiculous things. My dad would find out from my grandmother that I was lying, but he wouldn't totally believe her. He'd come back to me, not knowing whether to believe her or me.

Running Away

About that time, one of my friends was killed in a train station by a guy I thought was my friend. After that, he wanted to kill me too. I found myself in a lot of trouble with this guy over money and drugs and other stuff. It was so scary. I was glad when the guy finally went to jail and I could walk around again, but there were still other people out there to worry about.

Hiding from him and from other people became a problem for me. I couldn't tell my parents about it either. So I went to Chicago after that. It was actually my grandfather's decision; he didn't know someone was after me, he just knew I was always in trouble. So he asked me what I wanted to do with my life, if there was somewhere I wanted to go. I said no, but that I would really love to just get out of this city. So he said he thought I should go to Chicago and live with my uncle for a while.

I never really made friends there. I stayed with my uncle and worked for him. I'd leave the house early in the morning and my cousins would go to school. We would drop off one cousin on the South Side, and then go to work. We worked at a car dealership, and it was a really cool job for me. I learned everything about cars and got to drive all the time. My uncle would tell me all about my dad. I spent almost two years there before I moved back to Detroit.

Looking for Trouble

It was weird when I came back because people hadn't seen me for a while. I met a lot of people who knew what I had done and told me they didn't want to see me around again. I saw the guy who killed my friend. I felt really bad seeing him and was tempted to do something stupid, but I didn't. A lot of people who didn't know how much trouble I'd been in still wanted to hang out with me, but I was too scared of what might happen.

I moved back in with my parents, who were both trying to go to school. My dad made it through, but my mom didn't; she was too busy helping my dad. I had my room, though I barely lived there; I just came home to sleep. They didn't know what I was doing. I spent most of my time selling drugs downtown. I'd come home at five in the morning to go to sleep as they were leaving for work. Sometimes I wouldn't come home for months.

Then I got caught stealing cars. My father couldn't understand why I was doing all this stuff. Neither did I. I just thought it was cool. I kept getting into trouble and the police would call my home. As I got older, they stopped calling home and just started putting me in jail. When I'd finally show up at home, my mother would be in tears. After a while, she stopped crying, but she didn't really stop caring. She just got fed up and gave up.

I remember going to this guy's house. I was selling him drugs and I saw a kid come into the room in just a

diaper, walking on a ghetto-type wooden floor with the nails poking up. I saw these little kids eating cereal with water and watching TV while this guy was sitting there smoking drugs in front of them. I started crying and couldn't stop. I just left all the drugs there and went outside. I smoked cigarette after cigarette, and then I went back in to get my stuff, but half of it was gone. I just wanted to smack the guy. I went out onto the balcony and kept thinking that I had to change. I felt as if I were the one doing the drugs, like I was the crackhead. I left his house with the guy yelling at me. I saw his wife and told her she needed to get out of there. I gave her twenty dollars, which was all I could spare. I called Children's Services on this guy. I felt guilty because I knew it was none of my business how he was living his life, but I felt it was my business because I knew children's needs mattered too.

I went home to my parents. I got a job, and although I never kept one for longer than a couple of months, I was never without one again. My parents said that if I couldn't stick with one job, I was really unstable. They were so disappointed in me. They believed I was still selling drugs, especially when I had a night job. I tried to convince them I wasn't but they didn't believe me. They just didn't understand me, period.

After a while, I went back to the streets and started selling drugs again, for two months. Then I moved into a shelter for the first time in my life. I stayed there briefly, then I was kicked out for being high. I left there and went to many other shelters, trying to find out what I wanted to do. Last year, I went to a group home and I learned how to live in a house, get a job, do dishes. Sometimes I'd leave my dishes and the other residents would be yelling at me. Other times, I'd do my dishes but somebody else wouldn't,

and I'd be yelling at them. I was really learning how to live life in a house.

I liked having a place where things slowed down a bit and I was able to take my time to make some decisions. I met a lot of nice people, nice counselors. I told a few people what I'd been through and they were amazed at all the stuff.

At the house, I got into a film program they had for us to learn some new skills. One time I met a police officer who came in to talk to us about doing some wrestling films. He knew me from my bad times and was glad to see me volunteering to work on the film. He was totally on my case, but not for long. It didn't take him long to loosen up. The counselors talked to him, then asked me if it was okay if we all sat down and talked about my past. After hearing all the details, they said they were amazed I'd even made it to where I was, that I shouldn't even have been alive.

After that, I moved into another house. I was trying to get into the regular routine of having a job, so I tried to get up early. It was hard, though, because the people I lived with were noisy and smoking and high at night. Once, I had a job interview, so I decided to stay up the entire night before, but I fell asleep and ended up being half an hour late. I called and was told not to bother coming at all. I couldn't stand that so I just ran there. I arrived looking like I'd just woken up. But when I got there I was interviewed anyway. I thought I wouldn't get the job, but I was told I was the only one who was right for it. I've been there for eight months now! And I've got my own place. But I'm trying to take things one day at a time because I don't want to get back into trouble.

Looking Back

Looking back, my behavior at my grandparents' house was an example of what not to do. My grandfather used to try to scare me by telling me horror stories of what could happen to me out in the world if I stayed out really late. He was so angry, always yelling at me. My cousins used to ask me what it felt like to always be in trouble. At times, I'd be angry and I would take it out on someone else. I was never one to hit people, but if somebody hit me first I'd hit back, and then I'd get in trouble for it. A lot of times I felt that my birth had been a big mistake, that I was an inconvenience and I was messing up everyone else's lives. I learned later that I was screwing up so badly that one of my cousins would look at what I had done and try her hardest not to do the same.

My advice to other kids who have a childhood similar to mine would be to take their time and relax; to understand that there are a lot more things out there than just hanging out. Don't rush anything. I rushed into drugs and stuff. I didn't analyze, I just jumped into it. I remember my father telling me to take my time, and I thought it was stupid. It wasn't.

When I have kids, I think I'm going to be more open-minded than my father was. I'll listen to them attentively. When they see that, they'll know they can get attention from me, and that's important. I'll never be too busy for them.

If my kid got into trouble, the first thing I'd want to tell him is that I'd be there for him, whatever he did. I'd explain the same things to him that my father explained to me, and I'd tell him that it was advice passed down to me. I'd want him to be allowed to be whoever he wants to be. I'd want him to know that he could come to me.

Geri

Geri wonders what her life would have been like if her dad hadn't died when she was two years old. Maybe together her parents could have given her family the consistency that her mom couldn't provide on her own. It's possible that Geri wouldn't have caused so many problems, including being arrested three times for shoplifting, drugs, and assault. She thinks things are going to work out in the end, and she has gone back to school with plans to go on to college. Her advice to other kids: remember that your mom probably loves you, even if it's not easy to see it all the time. And don't get into trouble to look cool.

Without a Father

My life would have been very different if my dad had lived. He died of cancer when I was two, but if he'd lived, I don't think I would have done anything wrong. I would have lived in a big house and had a nine o'clock curfew. I'd probably have a car too.

My mom was a single parent to my older half-brother, my sisters and me: my brother is twenty-seven, Jasmine is eighteen, Shareen is fifteen, and I'm sixteen now. Her marriage history is a little complex. She was first married to my half-brother's father. After they divorced she married my dad and he legally adopted my half-brother. They had three daughters together before my dad died. My mom got married again, for about two years, to a real jerk. I don't even remember him, because I was only about five then.

My mom has gone out with a few different guys,

most of them jerks. She says she's attracted to jerks, that the only guy she ever went out with who wasn't one was my dad. She goes out with the "I watch sports, and I like to golf, and you have to make me my meals because I'm the man" types. She likes guys who take her out and stuff; they definitely wear the pants. They were always nice to me, though. My mom's one of those women who won't go out with anybody her kids don't like. She's good that way. She would never choose a guy over her daughters.

I think I'm my mom's favorite, but I get into lots of trouble with her. She says it's because I remind her of herself, which is weird, because my mom was never in trouble, and I've gotten into lots of trouble. She took me to counseling once and the therapist said that things would always be screwed up between us because my mom had been adopted and she hadn't worked that out. The shrink said my mom resents me, because even when I screw up she still loves me. I know that, so I do whatever I want — and she doesn't like me for that. It makes sense, because my mom always tells me that she got straight A's and never screwed up because she was afraid her parents would abandon her.

The Favorite Child

I guess there's always somebody in the family who gets away with everything. That's my older sister, Jasmine. She's so smart, she skipped three grades, so when she started screwing up, Mom didn't want to believe it. Jasmine was really cool even back when she was twelve; she did ecstasy and stuff when raves started. But she got addicted to heroin for more than a year when she was fifteen and sixteen. She had a boyfriend who moved in, and they lived together and started doing heroin. At first I thought it was cocaine because it was white powder and

she did it up her nose. Then I figured out it was heroin. She told me never to tell and I said I wouldn't, but then we got into a big fight and I yelled at her that at least I wasn't a heroin addict.

I tried to tell my mom about Jasmine but she thought I was lying. She didn't want to believe that her scholar-child was a heroin addict. She said I was making it up because I knew how happy she was about Jasmine and I knew she wasn't happy with me. I knew it was true, though, because she did it in front of me.

Two months later, my mom found heroin on a mirror. Jasmine told her it was ecstasy from the previous Halloween when she'd had friends over. My mom was so stupid, she said that was okay. Jasmine had been stealing money from her all the time, and my mom had been blaming me. Then she stole five hundred dollars from my mom's bank account and got caught. Finally, my mom knew the truth.

Jasmine is getting help now. She went for a drug test to get ready for methadone treatments and it came up that she was pregnant too. So she had an abortion, then started on the methadone. She's living at home too. She wanted to move out, so my mom gave her a hundred dollars for an agency to find apartment ads for her. If you follow up with their referrals, you get the money back when you find a place. Well, she didn't follow up and she lost my mom's money — but that was okay because she's Jasmine. She's allowed to do whatever she wants.

The Problem Child

My mom won't give *me* any money. She thinks I'm a criminal and a liar. Actually, I have been in some trouble with the cops. I've been arrested three times. But that's no reason to treat me so differently than my sister.

The first time I got arrested was for shoplifting, when I was twelve. I stole some expensive jackets from the mall. I was with another girl and we had been stealing stuff that entire day. We kept running and stashing everything in a locker, and then we'd go back and get more. After the first time I got away with it, I figured it was easy, and we could steal everything all the time. So we just kept at it. I had already stashed two jackets and was going back for a third, when, halfway up the escalator, this woman security guard grabbed us and told us we were under arrest for shoplifting. My friend and I just started hitting her to try to get away. She kicked the guard in the head and got away, but I was already in handcuffs. I got three charges: theft under five thousand, possession under five thousand, and assault with intent to resist arrest.

They called my mother, and she was so mad she called my brother to go and get me. But *he* was so mad he called his best friend to do it. I was wearing stolen pants, so the cops told him to bring me a pair of pants to wear home. He brought me the ugliest pants in the whole world — green with red paint stains on them. He made me walk through the mall in them, and then he drove me home. My mom said: "Oh…my…god! My daughter's a criminal!" Then she grounded me.

From then on, everything bad that ever happened at home was considered to be my fault. I'm not one of those whining girls who just imagines she's being blamed all the time. It was really like that. I guess because I was the first one to get in trouble by getting arrested, my mom just assumed any trouble at home must have been my doing.

I got arrested again for possession of a restricted weapon. It was because we were in a car and we picked up some guy. The cops pulled us over and the guy had a gun, but I was charged too, just because I was present. That

gave them a reason to search me, and I had some weed, so they charged me with that and dropped the weapon charge. My mom told me that I was horrible *and* she was going to kill me *and* I was going to go to jail for the rest of my life.

Each time I was arrested, she would kick me out. But it was kind of a joke. One minute she'd kick me out, then she'd ask me to move back, then she'd tell me that I wasn't allowed to leave. Until, of course, she kicked me out again!

About that time, my sisters started getting into trouble too. Jasmine got arrested for shoplifting from a drugstore and Shareen got arrested for assault. She was in the park with one of her friends and her friend beat up a girl, so she was charged too. At that point, my mom started to realize that lots of people get arrested, and that most teenagers get arrested for stealing something, sometime.

Then I got arrested for the third time. This time it was assault. My mom told me to get out of the house again, so I finally said "Screw you!" and I left. I mean, she kicked me out every week. It was ridiculous. I wasn't going to school, and I had only two credits from my third year of high school. So I decided that wasn't going to work for me. I told my mom I'd be moving out for good as soon as I could legally collect welfare.

Moving Out

As soon as I turned sixteen, I left home and got student welfare. I had to be in school to get it, so I went to school and was doing really well. I had an apartment for a couple of months, but I would still go back to the house because there was a TV there, something to do. After a while, my mom said if I was going to hang out there I should move back. I said no because she'd just kick me out again, but

she said she wouldn't, so I gave up my apartment and moved home. Two days later, what did she do? She kicked me out again. I said, "I hate you forever!" and I went to stay at my friend's. But of course my mom found out where I had gone and got me to move back home again.

Every time I got kicked out I'd call Shareen and ask her to meet me somewhere and bring me some clothes. Or I'd ask her to leave the back door unlocked so I could sneak into the house. My younger sister is so cool; she's the best. She doesn't get into real trouble. She's had the one assault charge, but that was because she was with a dumb girl who took another girl's bag. I don't even think she hit her. Shareen gets straight A's and she always comes home at a reasonable hour.

Sometimes I do have to protect her when she gets into trouble outside our home. Once she called me at four o'clock in the morning, saying she had started a fight with six huge girls, and she asked me to come and get her. I went in my pajamas with a butcher knife, and I told them I'd kill them if they ever bothered my sister again. They left. I don't think they were going to pick a fight with me. I looked crazy: I was in pajamas and flip-flops, and I was pissed off.

When Shareen does get into trouble at home, I usually take the blame for it. I do it because I know my mom is going to assume it's me anyway, so why get Shareen in trouble? I'm used to it. My mom doesn't even yell at me anymore. With Shareen, she still makes an effort. She'll get mad and yell so Shareen won't do it again. With me, my mom just says, "Oh, you did that."

Shareen and Jasmine hate each other. They fight worse than Jasmine and I do. I'm at the point where all I say to Jasmine is hi. I don't talk to her. But she and Shareen fight. Shareen will argue with her because she's

at the age where it's a power-trip thing. She'll say, "Screw you, you stupid ho!" I tell Shareen to shut up but she says, "No! She's a bitch! I'm gonna kill her!" and I have to hold her back.

A lot of the arguments in our house are about how my mom does or doesn't get along with the three of us. And it changes from day to day. Sometimes it's really confusing. My sisters usually get along with her a lot better than I do. They don't fight as much. Especially my mom and Jasmine. She's such a sneaky little brat. We never got along, even when we were little.

For instance, if my mom knows I did something wrong, she'll send Jasmine to soften me up. Jasmine will be friendly to me for about a week, then she'll try to get information out of me. As soon as I tell her, she'll run back to my mom and say, "Yeah, she did it. She just told me she did." Then my mom will come downstairs and say she heard me on the phone telling one of my friends something. I'll tell her that I know Jasmine told her, but she denies it.

Or my mom will go away and tell us not to have anybody over. Jasmine will have five people over, and I'll only have one, but she'll sneak to the phone and call my mom and tell her I have somebody over. She's such a rat. But it doesn't bug me that she doesn't get in trouble with my mom because I don't think my mom really likes Jasmine. I think she overcompensates because she feels guilty about that. I can tell. Nobody likes Jasmine. She doesn't have a good personality. If she weren't my sister I really wouldn't like her.

Bad Girls

I don't know why we are the way we are — Jasmine with her heroin addiction, me with my assault charge, and

Shareen getting charged. We were taught the difference between right and wrong. We just do the wrong thing anyway.

I think I got into stealing at first just because I wanted this really nice jacket. I don't know. My mom took me to a shrink and he said, "Why are you stealing? What do you need from life that makes you steal?" I set him straight right away. I told him I'm not one of those people who steal for attention, that when I want attention, I just ask for it. I actually wanted the jacket, and I knew my mom wasn't going to spend two hundred and fifty dollars on it. So I stole it.

Some people might say that we get into trouble because my mom didn't set strict-enough rules, but I don't think that's it. My mom was always really open about sex and everything. She has let me smoke in the house since I was about fifteen. I smoke her cigarettes and she smokes mine. She doesn't mind if I go out and drink, but she doesn't like me sitting around the house drinking beer with my friends. I haven't had a curfew in three years.

I think she's lax about the rules because she knows we're not like other kids. I'm not a naive sixteen-year-old girl who's careless and gets robbed on the streets. So I don't think she's too lenient. I've never been so drunk that I've puked, or fallen down in the street, but I think that's because she was so open. She'd say, "Here's some wine. Do you want some?" It was always around and I had access to it. But she never gave me more freedom than I could handle.

Some might say we're in trouble because when we were little we always had a nanny. I don't think that's the problem either. We loved our nannies and we still see them all the time. We used to go sleep there on the weekends. I don't have a problem with having been raised by nannies.

I don't think there's anything wrong with it. A person can only be a mother so much of the time.

I could have talked to my mom about stuff when I was growing up but I didn't want to. My mom knew we wouldn't come to her to ask for money to buy birth control so she put ten dollars in a jar and told us if any of us needed it, we should use it. She knew that we'd go without before asking her. That was pretty cool. She's like that.

It's not like I didn't have anyone to talk to, though. I talked with the youth staff at a community center, and I always had some good friends to talk to. When I used to get kicked out, I'd call my friend's mom. She'd say, "How much stuff do you have?" I'd answer, "Tons," and she'd say, "Okay, take a taxi and I'll pay for it." She always told me to come over if my mom and I were arguing.

Looking Back

I think my family is crazy. Although I always knew my mom loved me, she never showed any consistency, and I think that's something you need to have when you're raising a family. Her problem was that she was always switching back and forth, and I think that's probably what screwed up my family. It was a joke whenever my mom told me I was grounded. She never successfully grounded me in my entire life. She'd say, "Why should I ground you? I don't want to see you, so why would I want to make you stay around here?" She'd rather kick me out of the house. There were no curfews and no consistent punishments.

Now when she asks me to do something, I just do it out of respect, not because I have to. I know she feels better when she thinks she has some control over me. So I do what she wants because it makes her feel better. She's an old woman. She's fifty-three.

I think the way I grew up made me a more realistic person. I know life's not easy. I'm sixteen and I've already lived on my own. I'm going back to high school and, if I get through that, I want to go to college. But I don't know what I'm going to do with my life. I'm not going to move out on my own now because it costs too much money. And if my mom decides to kick me out again, I'm just not going to leave. I'll tell her that she always asks me to come back, so I'm not even going to bother leaving.

Overall, I think I'd raise my kids in the same open way my mom raised me. I think my sisters and I are okay, and I don't think we'll ever end up doing anything really bad. I definitely don't want to be the kind of mother who says you aren't allowed to have people over, or you have to be home by eleven, when all your friends are allowed out until one. It's so embarrassing to have to call your mother. I'd just be more consistent, that's all.

There are two things I always say as advice to my little sister's friends. Number one is that it's not cool to get in trouble, despite what you might think when you're younger. It's not cool to get arrested; for one thing, you get a record, and you can't travel anywhere if you've been convicted of a drug charge. I used to be eager to do bad stuff, but although something might seem like the cool thing to do at the time, you should think about the aftereffects. Number two is that, even though you may think she's trying to ruin your life, remember that your mother really does love you.

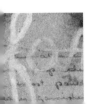

Logan

Logan has had a hard time getting along with his family for years. He was raised in a strict Christian household, where his parents thought it was important that he receive physical punishment. He left home and lived on the streets, where he found a life of drugs and violence. Through it all, he had loyal friends who supported him and watched out for him. His advice is to make and keep good friends, and look for the positive elements in your life.

Living With Violence

My family consists of my mom, my dad, my older sister and me. I grew up in the welfare projects, even though we weren't on welfare; both my parents worked. But my family isn't normal. We have some pretty big quirks, like the fact that my parents are hard-core born-again Christians. We went to church a lot, but their views on Christianity are twisted.

All "born-again Christian" means is that you have recommitted yourself to Christ. But my parents took the "don't spare the rod" thing very seriously. They hit my sister and me a lot "because they loved us." No particular incident comes to mind, because it was constant: whenever I did anything wrong, I got hit. One effect of all of these incidents was that my sister and I turned on each other.

It was embarrassing being in such an openly religious environment — like when they would insist on saying grace in a restaurant, for example. I was eventually able to tell them that I didn't feel comfortable with so much religious display, but it took a while.

Actually, I didn't tell them, I showed them, through rebellious acts, like not going to school, or smashing their car in retaliation for freaking out on me for being late once. That time, my mom hit me with a big metal spoon, and I hit her back with my fist. I was tired of being hit in the face for so many years. Then my dad put me up against the wall in a choke-hold.

There wasn't any drinking at my house. When my parents found out I was drinking, just experimenting, really, my mom said I was going to be just like her dad and beat my children. I guess she was scared. I said no, I wouldn't turn into some crazy guy from the 1940s, but she insisted that I would. Then she'd start on me about my needing to find God.

Later, near the point where I got kicked out of the house, I thought about actually going to the police and having my parents charged for all the physical stuff they did to me. I threatened to, but they said to go ahead, that it would be their word against mine, and nobody would believe me. That was always their attitude toward me, that top-authority, we-know-everything mentality.

I knew growing up that their way wasn't normal because I saw other parents treating their kids in a way that was totally cool: letting them do what they wanted, but disciplining them too, just more gently. I often felt confused by the craziness, and wondered where my normal life was.

Nowhere to Turn

My sister is actually my half-sister; her father left when she was four. He had Tourette's syndrome and so does she.

Tourette's is different for women. It's not just swearing, it's violent outbursts. My parents told me that from the time she was really young my sister would just walk up and kick people, then run away. She and I had all-out murder matches. I came at her with a butcher knife once; she came at me with a big hammer. I did it because of the build-up of past incidents. Maybe it's because of the Tourette's, but she was just constantly mean and sarcastic. I never really thought about the Tourette's; I just wondered why she was always such a bitch.

We get along better now. I think the Tourette's may have leveled off with her. With guys, it's different; it stays. Some women can just carry the gene and pass it on to their male children, but some experience a degree of it them-selves. It was suggested that my sister take medication but my mom said no, because she knew about the effects of those drugs from living with her first husband.

There was only one teacher I could talk to. It was when I was in the ninth grade. She was a friend of my mom's, but a cool chick at the same time, and she talked to me sometimes. She was my English teacher and she said I was her favorite student because I always debated different aspects of literature with her. I didn't go to her with my problems, but she could tell that I had some, just from knowing me. She noticed that I started doing drugs too, but she didn't say anything. My friends were normal teenagers, but even they started saying I was weird because I was doing so many drugs.

Living on the Street

As I said, one night I got back at my parents by bashing their car. A few days later, I got thrown out of the house, not because of that particular incident but because my parents were very erratic. It was sudden, but I was fine with it. I packed a bag and left, and I went on student welfare. I stayed at my friend's place and went to school for a while, and I tried to maintain a structured life of some sort. Then I met people downtown who could empathize with me because they came from similar backgrounds. They weren't people on the street, but people from a club I started going to. I liked the fact that these people just pretty much did whatever they wanted. They were older than me, but happy to have a cool kid around. I had no support from a welfare social worker or anything. They just told me not to miss three days of school or they'd cut me off.

I just always slipped through the cracks. I sold drugs, in massive quantities, for a long time. I've never been arrested. I had decided that normal work wasn't good, that it was just pointless, going nowhere. I knew the right people, and they hooked me up. They trusted me right away, which was a little too much responsibility for a fifteen-year-old. I was using and dealing. At first, I wasn't doing hard drugs, I was just smoking pot and doing acid, and drinking a lot, but I was selling massive quantities of acid and PCP at the club. I was still going to school at that point.

Then I dropped out and moved in with a guy downtown. He was really cool. I was sixteen by then. I wasn't having any contact with my parents or my sister. She had also been kicked out when she was fifteen. She just moved in with her boyfriend and got a job. She'd stop by home here and there. It's only within the last year and a half that I have resumed a relationship with her.

So I had quit school and was living with this older guy downtown, dealing and using drugs, and hanging out with a large circle of friends. It continued that way for a long time. No one had a problem with me. I had lots of money and, within my circle of friends, there were people with different political opinions, about the city and the government, so I got into that. I was in an anti-Fascist league for a little while. I kept informed about what was going on around me. But when I really started looking at things, I'd get really negative about it. Everywhere I looked, I saw corruption. It pissed me off, but I felt that one person alone couldn't do anything about it. So I tried to escape by doing a lot of drugs. I felt that if I had to live here, then I didn't want to deal with it.

I've been lucky in some ways, but unlucky in others. At one point, in a case of mistaken identity, I was stabbed by a bunch of guys. I was at Main Street Market Square. I was sitting in a little horseshoe thing there with my friend. I think they were after him, because they said, "What's up now, man?" and hit him first, but then they came after me.

I got a bunch of slashings across my leg. I went to a restaurant, bleeding seemingly from every part of my body, and some yuppie jerk told me to call a cab. I said, "Use your damn cell phone! Call an ambulance, you ass-hole!" So someone did. My friend ended up in the hospital for three weeks because his lung was punctured with a butcher knife. The police never caught the guys who did it. But we did.

Another time, I got hit by a car; I was a pedestrian, crossing on a green light. I was in a coma for four days, so the hospital called my family. They were there when I woke up. That was a little frightening. I was in the hospital for a week, and then I went home with them for six months. That was the only point when my family supported me. They let me move back home, but I noticed their mentality was still pretty much the same.

The car accident really screwed me up. I had a compound fracture in my left tibia; it popped out of my leg. I also had a hairline fracture in my pelvis, a head injury, and a back injury. I didn't walk for six months.

It was weird. My family took care of me, but there was all this lawyer stuff. As soon as I could walk, I wanted out of there. They said I'd just go back to doing drugs, but all I thought was that they didn't even know me.

By then they weren't hitting me anymore, because they knew I would have killed them. Instead, they were just messing with my head. I don't know the terminology for it, I just know my mom. She really knows how to talk down to someone. She asks you a question, but never gives you the chance to answer. She doesn't really want to hear what you have to say.

So I left as soon as I could and went back downtown. I'd had an apartment, off and on, not because I was irresponsible, but because sometimes I just wouldn't feel like paying rent to some landlord, and a park would look inviting, so I'd just hang out on the streets. I'd get hassled a lot by cops, but I think I was just really lucky, because I was carrying a lot of stuff and I never got arrested.

Steps to Recovery

I got $40,000 as a settlement from the accident and I spent it in three weeks, on everything from crack to heroin. When I got down to my last $20, I had a nervous breakdown. So I checked out a rehabilitation place that I'd heard about from a girl on the street, and luckily they had prompt admission. If they'd had a waiting list, I probably wouldn't have gone. There's a two-week period to process paperwork, but they pretty much take you right away.

My parents drove me there. The rehab center was the place where I started building a real relationship with them, over the phone. We would call each other. That was when I started being really straightforward with them. I told them they had to change, and they had to stop pushing their views on me; that they had to stop being over-

bearing and talking to me like I was a kid, or they were never going to see me again. And they did change. Now they treat me with respect, and I treat them with respect.

My sister has her own life, and now we laugh about how we used to try to kill each other. We don't discuss too much about our past, because she had a huge hate-on for my dad, and I hated my mom. I sort of like my dad, and she likes my mom. I liked my dad because he never really said much. He's always been a tranquil guy, except when you get him pissed. He's always got his hands in his pockets and his pipe hanging out of his mouth. But my mom is wound up. She's a corporate-executive Christian who was raised in the '40s by an alcoholic family and beaten her whole life.

It's okay living back there with them now, because they respect my space and I respect theirs. I don't see much of them. We eat dinner together once in a while, but it's just a temporary arrangement anyway. I'm getting my own place again soon.

After the Craziness

My life is much calmer now, though I still go out and party. The only aspect of living on the streets that I miss is the absolute freedom: there was a time when I would just head off to Seattle, just because I could. Now I have a job, at a social services agency, so I'm more tied down, but it's okay.

My advice to other kids experiencing anything similar to my life is, first, to make friends, and, second, not to mistreat them. If you've already screwed things up with your family, and then you screw over your friends, you're going to be alone, just a crackhead in the streets. You see those guys walking around, looking like they're thirty-five years old, and they're just complete crackheads. Or they're insane, wearing those psychiatric hospital wristbands.

Having friends kept me stable. I have really good friends, and not all of them did drugs. They accepted the fact that I did drugs; I guess they had a higher level of tolerance than most people, because they hung out with me anyway.

I'd advise other kids who live in a violent home to stop hiding it. Tell your parents, or tell someone else, when someone, or something, is bothering you. I threatened my parents with calling the cops on them, but I didn't do it. I should have, but I actually believed their bullshit when they said that no one would believe me.

I don't think about the past very much. I just think about the present, and how to improve my life now. I'm not one of those people, like a typical psychologist, who blames things I'm going through now on the past. Neither does the place I work for. That's why I decided to work for it, because they have a good mentality.

I always saw the negative, but I saw the positive too, so I guess you could say my brain was a living yin-yang. I focused on the negative a lot, but I always knew there was a positive. I just chose to ignore it for a long time.

Aislin

Aislin had to deal with a lot. When her father drank, he was abusive and unpredictable. Her mother was never there for her and refused to acknowledge that she was being sexually abused. But thanks in part to the special interest paid by an eighth-grade teacher, Aislin started looking at herself and her family in a different way. Exploring her artistic talent gave her a creative outlet and allowed her to re-examine her strengths and put things into perspective. Her advice to kids going through tough times: trust yourself and find ways of building on your strengths.

Dad's An Alcoholic

When I was ten, my dad was dealing with alcoholism. He didn't drink in the house much, but he often went out after work and drank. My mom was always worried because he never called and she never knew where he was. That freaked us all out a bit.

He always drank and drove. Always. Sometimes I was in the car too, but mostly it was just him. I was always aware of the danger of his drinking and driving. I knew that he could totally die from doing that, so it was pretty scary.

When my dad came home after drinking, it would be one of two extremes: He might be really happy, which wasn't good for me because he'd come and bug me. He didn't really get along with my mother. He just didn't have any interest in her. So he would come into my room in the middle of the night and wake me up and start tickling me, or wrestling with me, or kissing me. He always used to do that, and I would get so angry, but I never said anything. One time, though, he was bugging me, kissing me all over my face, and totally out of the blue, I yelled at him: "Stop kissing me!" He got so mad, he went downstairs and stormed out of the house. He was so pissed off at me that I thought I had done something totally wrong and I felt really guilty. I was about twelve then.

My brother and sister-in-law moved into the house for about a year when I was twelve. They were about twenty at the time. I remember my sister-in-law coming into my room and telling my father to leave me alone, telling him he was drunk and he should just get out of there. So she kind of protected me in the time that she was there. My mom never said anything, even though I think she knew what was going on.

The other extreme was that he would come home after a night of drinking and the littlest thing would set him off. He never physically hit me or my mother, but he was violent with the inanimate objects around him. He would throw his toolboxes downstairs, or something like that.

I tried to make him promise he wouldn't drink and drive anymore, but he continually broke his promise. That pissed me off. There were also times when he would get upset about his own life and he would ignore me for weeks. He would be so cold and mean. It would kill me. I'd just go crazy when he did that.

There were lots of ways that I acted out during those times. I used to fake-injure myself. Maybe I was following in my mother's footsteps; she was a bit of a hypochondriac too. I'd smash my arm against the pavement until it was all screwed up and needed a cast, just to get attention. But I did stuff like that so often that I don't think it worked. I would fake laryngitis for three weeks, but I'd still go to

school. I wasn't doing it to get out of school; I was doing it for attention.

I also started drinking and smoking weed at a really young age. The first time I got drunk I was in grade two. The second time was in grade seven. I used to take care of some kids during lunchtime, and while I was there I drank all this booze and went back to school and vomited everywhere. I smoked my first joint when I was in the eighth grade.

An Absent Mother

I never see my mom in any of my memories. I know she was probably in the house, because she was usually there when I was, but she wasn't really around. I think my mom lives totally in her head: she can make up all these things and that becomes her reality.

When I was younger, she managed a convenience store, and she once dropped a huge CO_2 tank on her foot and had to go into a rehab clinic for eight weeks. My father took care of me during that time. She also had a lot of cancer scares, and she was in the hospital for that, until she finally had a hysterectomy. The clearest memory I have of her was after she had her breast reduction done. There was a nurse who came to clean her wounds for the first couple of weeks, and then my mother was supposed to do it herself. But it was hard for her to see what she was doing, so I had to do it and it totally freaked me out. She had these huge scars on her breasts. Just seeing her naked was difficult for me, much less having to see the scars and touch them.

There was a serious division in my family. It was my father and me against my mother. I was never very close to her. She was in pain a lot of the time, but I never thought of it that way. I just saw her as a woman who complained all the time, and I didn't want to be around her. My father and I used to take off for long walks together. I remember coming back home one really sunny day to find her sitting outside. She was upset. We told her about all we had done, and she said, "You guys never stay here and do anything with me." I just snapped at her, "Why would I want to sit here and listen to you complain all the time!" I still feel guilty about that. I was totally insensitive to what she was going through. But there wasn't really anyone taking care of me a lot of the time.

I couldn't talk to my father about how I felt about my mom because he encouraged me to hate her. He didn't like her and he encouraged me to believe that she was an idiot who didn't know what she was talking about. I didn't feel manipulated at all at the time. I revered him; I thought he was the smartest man on the planet. I listened to him. I was involved in an art school, so I was exposed to different things, like music and literature. I brought that home and he got really interested in classical music and Russian literature and all these different things. So together we just started developing these intellectual interests, and I thought he was really smart, and a lot bigger than the life he was living.

A Fractured Family

My parents split up when I was seventeen. They don't talk much now. My mother is still civil to my father, in spite of the way he behaved towards me. I don't think it was her fault, but she didn't do anything to protect me either. I don't dwell on that, but I don't feel like I was mothered by her. As a kid, I never felt that anyone was protecting me. Even the people who were babysitting me when I was seven or eight were sexually abusing me. It seemed like there were bad people everywhere.

I could never talk to my brother either. He is more closed-up than anyone in my family. He doesn't want to hear about anything, or talk about anything. He can block you out like no one else can. My brother and I have a great amount of respect for each other, in terms of what we do and the people we are, but we don't have a close relationship. He's almost ten years older than me, so we were never close as kids. He moved to the East Coast for a year, then he moved back, to a city that's only an hour away from here, but to a kid who had no mode of transportation it was still hard to get there. So I was really dealing with my family on my own.

I have a pretty strong relationship with my grandfather now, but that's only been since my grandmother died, when I was seventeen. Since then, he has reached out, and been more affectionate, and talked more. I was close to my grandmother when she was alive. I really liked spending time with her. We'd have little tea parties and talk, but she had no idea what was going on in my family. My mother had left my father before she died, but my grandmother didn't know. There was total secrecy in our family. We never talked about anything.

My family went to church a lot, and until I was about eight both my parents were involved in the church. My mother had had a really strict Catholic upbringing; she went to an all-girl Catholic high school and wasn't allowed to date until she was eighteen.

My father wasn't from that background, but he started going to church when they were first married and we were young kids. I think he just did it for her. I went to a Catholic school that was right across the street from the church, so we went to church all the time, not just on Sundays. But the Catholic church never made sense to me. There was no comfort in it. If anything, it seemed threatening to me, a weird, controlling environment. By the time I was eight I was an atheist. I stopped going to church when I was twelve, but I had to go to a Catholic high school, so I still had to deal with the whole church thing. But it never supported me.

Seeing the Light

To a certain degree everything seemed fine to me until I was a teenager. I was fourteen or fifteen when I started thinking about things more. Then I really started to look at my parents. They would come home and sit in the same room, watching TV or reading the newspaper, and never say a word to each other. They never hugged or kissed or even spoke. And I suddenly realized that was kind of weird.

It was hard to see that my family was strange because my friends didn't have normal families either, though a few seemed a lot more ideal than mine. I think I figured it out on my own because I was pretty sensitive and aware. And I read a lot.

It was easier to realize that my father's alcoholism was a problem, because that was something society talked about; I had exposure to it outside the house. I remember when I was pretty young I tried to write in my journal to one of my teachers about the problems at home. We had journal-writing in class; the teacher would write the first sentence, and then we'd have to finish the paragraph. The first sentence he wrote this time was "The thing that scares me the most is…" and I continued it with "…my father will come home drunk when I have a friend over and he'll do something." But my teacher never said anything. I don't even know if he read it.

When I was in grade eight, I had a teacher, Mrs. Hatfield, who stands out in my life as the person who really cared about me, outside the family. I didn't really talk to her about what was going on with my family, but I was very honest about my feelings about everything else. She encouraged me to write poetry and to do positive things. She was really supportive about the art I did and the dreams I had, and she encouraged me to try hard. In the lower grades, I had never done very well on my report cards; I got C's and D's. But when I had Mrs. Hatfield I got straight A's. She encouraged me to work hard and to do well.

I think it was her influence that made me want to strive for a really big life. It probably pushed me to see that I needed to go beyond the boundaries laid down by my family.

Saved by Art

Having artistic talent is probably what saved me more than anything else. Until I was twelve, I just used to draw the things around me or copy pictures. But then I began to draw the things that were inside me. That was a total release and a way to cope with my life. I never saw those paintings as pure expressions of what I was going through; I didn't think that way then. But the paintings really are about that — a way to get it out and not feel so crazy. They were also something to be proud of because I was always better at it than almost anybody else. In high school, my art teachers were really encouraging and supportive. Even when I thought I was ugly and stupid, I always knew I was a good artist, so I didn't see my future as bleak. I thought I would be a famous artist. I don't know if I would be alive if I hadn't had that. I'm not exaggerating. Beyond being an emotional outlet, being an artist gave me something to look forward to, something to hope for. I just kept myself busy working toward that goal.

Looking Back

I used to obsess about how ugly or stupid I was. My parents hated themselves and each other, so I think I just never learned self-respect. I learned it later, by going to a therapist for three years and by being really honest about what had gone on at home. I learned to look past the bull-shit and see that all these things I do and say and tell myself are distractions, not the actual truth.

I would obsess about boys too, more than an ordinary girl would. I'd think I was so in love, and then be so crushed by them; it was a way to distract myself from what was going on. The only thing that's very clear about that period is that I know I didn't like myself at all. I used to write tons in journals, always about how much I didn't understand, about how ugly and stupid I was, and how some particular boy would never like me.

Lots of things happened in my teenage years that make it clear to me now that my family was not okay. My father went through spells of being angry and not talking to me. One night when he was really drunk he tried to start his car but couldn't, and it started sparking. He just kept trying and trying to start it, until the car actually blew up. His hair was all singed, but he was fine. That showed me he had serious problems.

My father also used to talk to me about having gone to prison a couple of times. I'm not sure why he went; what he told me was different from what he told my mom. He said he went to prison the first time because he stole a car. The second time, he said, was because he was buying and selling guns. He said he had broken into this place and stolen a gun that was extremely rare; he got caught when he tried to sell it because it was easily traceable. So he went to prison for a couple of years. This was before I was born.

He always told me stuff like that. He talked about all

the drugs he had used and how he'd broken into pharmacies and stolen all these pharmaceuticals, and how he had been chased by cops. He really glamorized that life and I saw it as very cool, until I was about fifteen. I smoked joints with my dad when I was underage. But eventually I started seeing that it wasn't so cool.

Coming Through

It's hard to come up with advice for other kids in similar situations. I don't know if you can tell twelve-year-olds to stay focused on themselves. That's what I would tell another adult, but that's it, really. Just trust yourself and acknowledge the way you feel, and focus on something constructive and positive, whether it's art or running or playing basketball or writing.

Other people always advise you to "talk about it." But in my own experience that never really happened. I guess talking about it might have helped me, at least, to be more aware of the burden I carried by looking after myself so much. I don't think I realized that then. I'm still not sure that I know how to take care of myself.

I think my family experience changed how I look at life. At times I was very pessimistic, and not trusting, especially as a young girl having boyfriends. I really couldn't have good relationships because I didn't trust them. I would act out and need them but hate them at the same time. Living in my family really messed up my ability to relate to people.

I've worked through that, but it still affects how I relate, especially with my male partner, and even with my female friends. I don't deal with conflict very well. I find it hard to speak up for myself, and be clear, and set boundaries with friends.

Everyone has issues, but I can clearly see how my

relationship problems stemmed from my parents. I some-times think of it as having lived in a vacuum from concep-tion. My friend and I joke about that sometimes, about where the hell I come in in the mix of this. I've always just gone with the feeling that I'm here to do something, and that there's a purpose to my life. I believe I had to experi-ence what I did to become strong enough to deal with the big things that I'm going to have to do with my talent.

Afterword

If you read this book you probably did so because you think your family is a little crazy. Some of these stories may sound just like your life. Reading about how other young people have coped with their family difficulties may have given you ideas for things you could try. However, some of their stories might have made you feel discouraged or think that there's no way you could solve a problem that seems to have gone on forever.

You may be very worried about your family or about yourself. When kids are fighting with parents or when parents are fighting with each other, kids can become anxious, afraid to go out or unable to do ordinary things like schoolwork. Some can get preoccupied with what they eat and think they need to diet or lose weight, and some turn to drugs and alcohol because it helps them forget what's going on in their families. All of these responses can make it hard for kids to make their lives work or to realize their dreams. Sometimes they become big problems that they can't overcome even as adults. Most of these things are signs that kids are feeling sad or angry.

Many of the young people in these stories had parents who were separated or divorced. Most kids who go through this experience end up feeling caught between their parents. Some even feel they have to be the "parent" to their parents. This can be very frustrating. All kids want their parents to be grown up and able to look after themselves as well as their kids. When parents go through a separation or divorce they often aren't functioning very well for a long time before and after the breakup. This can mean that they don't have the same time or energy for their kids that they used to. Sometimes it means that kids end up looking after themselves and their brothers and sisters.

This makes most kids pretty angry. If this is happening to you, it's important to let a parent know how you're feeling. Your parents may not realize how their behavior is making you feel. If your parents can't hear you, then it is important to try another adult who may be able to connect you with someone who can help.

Maybe you feel so angry about what's happening in your family that you have tried to show your parents how you feel. This may mean you have taken risks or done dangerous things as a way of getting adults to pay attention. The problem with this approach is that sometimes it doesn't work and you get hurt. It's always better to find someone who may be able to hear what is upsetting you and give them a chance to see if they can help or direct you to someone who can.

You may be feeling so frustrated with your family that you have thought about suicide. If you have grown up in a family where there is a lot of fighting, or where you or your sisters or brothers have experienced physical or sexual abuse, you may feel depressed or helpless. It's very common to think of suicide when you feel this way. But depression can be treated, and so it's important to discuss these feelings with an adult who can help.

Sometimes kids feel that no one could possibly help or understand their crazy family, and sometimes they feel that no one would care enough to talk to them. Although it's true that some families can't change, there are usually ways to help kids make their lives work better — if not with their family, then outside of it. Many of the kids in these stories had to live with other people because their families couldn't support them adequately, and this provided a new chance to get their lives back on track.

By now you've probably got the message: It's important to talk to someone about how you're feeling.

How to Find Help

You could start by showing this book to your parents and asking them to read it. Tell them you'd like to be able to talk to them about some of the things you've learned that might help the family get along better. It may surprise you that your parents would be interested in getting the family to work better. If they are interested in getting help there are a number of different agencies and people available to do this.

You could start with your family doctor or school guidance counselor. They can direct you to resources in your community, services that exist to help kids in difficult families. This includes programs for young people who are depressed, anxious or suicidal, who may have an eating disorder, drug or alcohol problem, or whose parents are separating or getting divorced. Your doctor or guidance counselor will treat what you say in a confidential way and can help you decide what to do and where to go for help. If you have trouble talking to your doctor or guidance counselor, perhaps you have a grandparent, aunt, uncle, neighbor or schoolteacher with whom you feel comfortable who could help you figure out how to get help.

If talking face-to-face is difficult, think about calling a hotline where you can explain what is happening and get advice about what is available in your community. Sometimes just talking to a person who understands what you're going through can make you feel less discouraged. Hotline numbers are usually posted in places like the bulletin board at your school, doctor's office, or community center. Again, these services are confidential and are especially helpful when you feel no one else is there for you.

In the United States you can call the National Runaway Switchboard at 1-800-621-4000 or Kids Peace HelpLine at 1-800-334-4KID.
In Canada, the Kids Help Phone can be reached by calling 1-800-668-6868.

If you like to use the Internet, there are many web sites that can give you more information. Here are some you can try: **In Canada** check out http://kidshelp.sympatico.ca.
In the United States you can reach the KidsPeace at http://www.teencentral.net or National Runaway Switchboard at http://www.nrscrisisline.org.

The kids in these stories tried different ways of getting help, and some got into trouble along the way. Those who got their lives back on track were usually able to find someone to talk to or some way of believing in themselves or their abilities. You may want to remind yourself of some of the things you do well and find time to work at them. We all need things that make us feel good about ourselves. For some this comes from knowing that others care; for others it comes from knowing that they can do something well and can hold on to a dream that when they grow up they will use their talents in a special way. We all need dreams. Dreams keep us working to make our lives the way we want them to be. So hold on to your dreams and don't hesitate to let someone know that you're not happy, if what's happening in your life doesn't make sense.

Dr. Susan Bradley
Professor, University of Toronto
Department of Psychiatry
The Hospital For Sick Children
Toronto, Canada